Federal Acquisition
Key Issues and Guidance

Federal Acquisition
Key Issues and Guidance

PAULA COMPTON

꧁ **MANAGEMENT**CONCEPTS

〔〔〔
MANAGEMENTCONCEPTS
8230 Leesburg Pike, Suite 800
Vienna, VA 22182
(703) 790-9595
Fax: (703) 790-1371
www.managementconcepts.com

Printed in the United States of America

Library of Congress Cataloging-in-Publication Data

Compton, Paula B.
    Federal acquisition : key issues and guidance / Paula B. Compton.
        p. cm.
    ISBN 978-1-56726-248-3
1. Government purchasing—United States. I. Title.
JK1673.C63 2009
352.5'30973—dc22

                                                                        2009038888

10   9   8   7   6   5   4   3   2   1

About the Author

Paula Compton has been involved in federal acquisitions with a number of U.S. government agencies for over 30 years. She has held staff and management positions in both operations and policy, in the United States and abroad. She is currently an independent consultant.

Paula received her bachelor's degree from the California State University, Northridge; a master's degree in architecture and urban planning from the University of California, Los Angeles; and a master's degree in public law from the Antioch School of Law (now the David A. Clarke School of Law).

Contents

Preface

The federal acquisition system is guided by many laws, regulations, and legal decisions that have set precedents for current and future acquisition practices and principles. Acquisition professionals within the federal government often need help to understand the complexities of the federal acquisition process. This book is intended to serve as a quick reference guide to key issues for professionals new to the field of federal acquisition and others who assist with acquisition actions. Seasoned acquisition professionals may want to use the book to refresh their knowledge of key issues.

Acquisition audit reports by the Government Accountability Office and the Office of the Inspector General for civilian and defense agencies often reveal that acquisition laws are not being followed when contracts are prepared, which leads to problems in the federal acquisition process. These reports consistently state that acquisition requirements are not adequately addressed, are not properly documented, or are omitted entirely from solicitations and contracts issued by the government.

I wrote this book to provide guidance and information on these essential acquisition processes. My goal is to help acquisition professionals follow the required laws and regulations when developing, awarding, and administering federal contracts.

To develop contracts that are legally binding and enforceable, certain processes must be followed. These processes form the skeleton of federal contracts. The reader is encouraged to become familiar with the topics in each chapter and to use them when developing federal contracts, keeping in mind that this book does not cover every element of the federal acquisition life cycle.

Acquisitions rules, regulations, and procedures often change. Therefore, every reader should verify information by consulting the most current version of the Federal Acquisition Regulation (FAR) when preparing federal contracts. It contains uniform policies and procedures and is the primary source of information on the acquisition of supplies and services for the federal government. The FAR can be found online at http://www.arnet.gov/far and http://farsite.hill.af.mil.

This book is divided into four parts:

- ◆ **Part I: The Acquisition Planning Phase** provides information on the essential elements of acquisition planning, including the preparation of required documents.

- ◆ **Part II: The Solicitation Phase** provides information on the required solicitation provisions and contract clauses, the proposal evaluation process, and legal review of the solicitation.

- ◆ **Part III: The Evaluation, Negotiation, and Award Phase** provides information on the purpose of and need for proposal evaluation, cost and price analysis, legal review of the award document, and notification of unsuccessful vendors.

- ◆ **Part IV: The Postaward Phase** provides information on the training and selection of the technical personnel who will monitor the contract, their duties and responsibilities, and when and how to exercise contract option periods.

Each part also includes sample acquisition templates based on the policies and procedures laid out in the FAR. I developed some of the templates and modified others used by various acquisition organizations so that they reflect the current FAR requirements. All these templates are in the public domain and can thus be used and modified freely. The templates are basic and simple in design so they can be modified to fit all types of acquisition actions.

Paula Compton
October 2009

Acknowledgments

Two people provided valuable assistance and contributed to the success of this book. I would like to thank Myra Strauss for reviewing the initial drafts and providing guidance in structuring the content of the book. I would also like to thank Courtney Chiaparas for providing valuable editing services.

Introduction

Every year the federal government spends billions of dollars on the acquisition of supplies and services to carry out its duties and responsibilities. The government uses complex acquisition policies and procedures to make these purchases. These policies and procedures are followed during each of the four phases of the federal acquisition process: the acquisition planning phase; the solicitation phase; the evaluation, negotiation, and award phase; and the postaward phase.

The acquisition planning phase is the first phase of the federal acquisition process. This phase is very important because it establishes the foundation of the contract. During the planning phase, the government must ensure that:

- Appropriated funds are available

- Proper cost estimates are prepared

- Sole source procurements are justified (when using noncompetitive procedures)

- Market research is performed

- The government's requirements are well defined in the statement of work

- The appropriate type of contract is selected for the acquisition

- Performance-based acquisition is employed (when acquiring services)

◆ Small business concerns are given an opportunity to obtain the contract.

When the required planning documents are of poor quality or are omitted from the planning process, the solicitation activities in the second phase of the acquisition process will be negatively affected. The planning process must be thorough, addressing each of the points above. Otherwise, the resulting contract may cost much more than budgeted for or may take longer to complete than expected. For example, if the government's cost estimate is inaccurate because it was poorly prepared, it will hinder the cost or price evaluation process. It may be useless in determining whether the proposed contract price is fair and reasonable. Conversely, well-planned and documented acquisition actions that are in compliance with laws and regulations will meet the government's needs in the most effective, economical, and timely manner.

The second phase of the federal acquisition process is the preparation of the solicitation and associated documentation. The solicitation must:

◆ Include the appropriate solicitation and contract provisions and clauses to be in compliance with applicable laws and regulations.

◆ Include the criteria to be used in the evaluation of vendor proposals. The technical evaluation criteria should be prepared with great care so that they fit the evaluation method to be used. Carefully chosen and documented criteria allow for the thorough and accurate evaluation of proposals, which is performed during the evaluation and negotiation phase of the acquisition process.

◆ Be legally sufficient before it is issued to the public. All solicitations beyond the simplified acquisition threshold must be reviewed for legal sufficiency. Legal review will ensure that the solicitation is in compliance with acquisition laws and is legally defensible in case of a protest.

The third phase of the federal acquisition process is the evaluation, negotiation, and award phase. Under the contracting by negotiation method, proposals are evaluated, and discussion and negotiations are held with vendors. This phase includes:

- **Evaluating proposals.** When an evaluation is not performed in accordance with the evaluation criteria specified in the solicitation, the Government Accountability Office will contest the evaluation and find it to be not fair or reasonable.

- **Determining vendors' price reasonableness and responsibility.**

- **Negotiating with competing vendors.** Negotiations must be held unless the solicitation states that the award will be made without discussion.

- **Reviewing the award document.** It is very important to have contracts reviewed for legal sufficiency prior to award to ensure that they are in compliance with the appropriate laws and regulations.

- **Awarding the contract.**

- **Announcing the contract award to the public.** This announcement should be made in accordance with policies established by the agency.

- **Notifying and debriefing unsuccessful vendors.** These vendors must be told why they were eliminated from competition or did not receive the contract award.

The fourth phase of the federal acquisition process is the postaward phase, sometimes called the contract administration phase. The goal of contract administration is to ensure that the government receives quality supplies or services that conform to the requirements of the contract in a timely manner.

To that end, certain postaward activities must be carried out properly for each acquisition. This includes training and certifying the contracting officer's technical representative to properly perform contract surveillance, which helps ensure that quality supplies or services are delivered to the government in a timely manner. This also includes exercising contract option periods in accordance with contract provisions and clauses. Option periods exercised by federal agencies must be in exact compliance with the option provisions and clauses of the contract.

Federal agencies too often allocate more time to awarding contracts than to the postaward phase of the acquisition process. The postaward phase is also very important, so it should receive the proper amount of resources and time.

PART I

The Acquisition Planning Phase

CHAPTER 1

Funding: The Availability of Appropriations and the Bona Fide Needs Rule

(FAR 32.7; Government Accountability Office, *Principles of Federal Appropriations Law,* Volumes I and II)

The first phase of the federal acquisition process is known as the *acquisition planning phase.* Understanding the rules that apply to federal appropriations is an important part of the planning phase—one that is too often neglected. Acquisition audit reports have identified many violations of the rules that pertain to federal appropriations. The audit reports indicate that some federal agencies do not adhere to the limitations on purpose, amount, and time. For example, an acquisition organization violated the purpose limitation by using a contract for computers and accessories to purchase army Humvees. Another organization violated the time and amount limitation by awarding a contract to purchase equipment for use in fiscal year 2005 with expired fiscal year 2004 funds.

It is essential, then, for every acquisition professional to understand that appropriations for federal agencies are made for specific purposes during specified fiscal years and that the funds may be obligated and expended only within the amounts appropriated by Congress. They must also understand that appropriated funds may be obligated only to meet a legitimate—or bona fide—need in the fiscal year(s) for which appropriation was made.

THE AVAILABILITY OF APPROPRIATIONS

The fiscal year for federal agencies begins on October 1 and ends on September 30 of the following year. Funds are provided to federal agencies through annual appropriations acts passed by Congress and approved by the president of the United States.

Appropriations acts make funds available to federal agencies for obligations. The funds are classified as annual, multiple-year (or multiyear), and no-year appropriations. *Annual* appropriations are available for obligation for one year; *multiple-year* appropriations are available for obligation for a certain period of time beyond one fiscal year. *No-year* appropriations are not limited to any fiscal year and are available for obligation for an indefinite period. The appropriations act for each agency identifies the function, amount, and purpose of the funding and the time frame for its use. Most agencies are allotted funding for functions such as operations and maintenance, procurement, research and development, and other functions within the agency.

These appropriations acts (also called *appropriations bills* or *appropriations legislation*) are supposed to be enacted by September 30 of each year so that agencies can be fully operational by October 1. Congress has not been able to pass the necessary appropriations for most civilian agencies in a timely manner for quite some time now. When appropriations acts are not passed by October 1, Congress passes a piece of legislation called a *continuing resolution,* which provides temporary budget authority so that agencies can continue operating until the appropriations are approved. A continuing resolution, which must be signed by the president, makes funds available until the resolution expires or annual appropriations acts are passed and enacted. During the continuing resolution period, funds are provided for one or two months at a time and at the same funding level as the previous year.

The 12 appropriations acts for fiscal year 2009 passed by Congress and signed by the president are listed in Exhibit 1-1. Federal departmental and nondepartmental agencies are listed under the 2009 appropriations acts that apply to them.

EXHIBIT 1-1: Federal Appropriations Acts in Fiscal Year 2009	
Agriculture, Rural Development, Food and Drug Administration, and Related Agencies Appropriations Act: • Department of Agriculture, excluding Forest Service • Department of Health and Human Services, excluding the Indian Health Service • Food and Drug Administration within the Department of Health and Human Services	**Department of the Interior, Environment, and Related Agencies Appropriations Act:** • Department of the Interior, excluding the Bureau of Reclamation • Forest Service, within the Department of Agriculture • Indian Health Service, within the Department of Health and Human Services • Environmental Protection Agency
Commerce, Justice, Science, and Related Agencies Appropriations Act: • Department of Commerce • Department of Justice • Department of State • National Aeronautics and Space Administration • National Science Foundation	**Department of Labor, Health and Human Services, and Education and Related Agencies Appropriations Act:** • Department of Labor • Department of Health and Human Services, excluding the Food and Drug Administration and the Indian Health Service • Department of Education • Social Security Administration
Department of Defense Appropriations Act	**Legislative Branch Appropriations Act**
Energy and Water Development and Related Agencies Appropriations Act: • Department of Energy • Corps of Engineers • Bureau of Reclamation within the Department of the Interior	**Military Construction and Veterans Affairs and Related Agencies Appropriations Act:** • Department of Defense, military construction • Department of Veterans Affairs
Financial Services and General Government Appropriations Act: • Department of the Treasury • District of Columbia • Executive Office of the President	**Department of State, Foreign Operations, and Related Programs Appropriations Act:** • Department of State • Agency for International Development

EXHIBIT 1-1: Federal Appropriations Acts in Fiscal Year 2009 (cont.)	
Department of Homeland Security Appropriations Act	**Transportation, Housing and Urban Development, and Related Agencies Appropriations Act:** • Department of Transportation • Department of Housing and Urban Development

LIMITATIONS ON APPROPRIATED FUNDS

Congress retains full control over appropriated funds by imposing three limitations that are related to purpose, time, and amount. These limitations restrict the amount of appropriated funds a federal agency can spend within a specified period of time and ensure that funds are spent only for the intended purpose. Funds for each fiscal year must be legally available for obligation or expenditure before an agency may purchase supplies or services. *Legally available* means that all three limitations—on purpose, time, and amount—must be satisfied. An obligation or expenditure for any given item is not legal if all three are not satisfied. Of the three, the purpose and time limitations are most frequently violated by acquisition organizations.

The Purpose Limitation

The statute for the purpose element (at 31 USC 1301(a)) reads:

> Appropriations shall be applied only to the objects for which the appropriations were made except as provided by law.

The statute clearly indicates that public funds may be used only for the purpose or purposes for which they were appropriated. The purpose language in an appropriations act is usually clear so that the agency can easily determine the purpose for which the funds are to be used. Nonetheless, sometimes the appropriation language is not clear or is too general to determine the purpose of the appropriation. In a situation like this, it is necessary for the agency to review both the legislation that authorized the program and the appropriations act that provided budget authority for the program to determine the purpose for which the funds may be used.

When an agency deliberately obligates funds from the wrong appropriation with the intent to later use the right appropriation, it violates the purpose statute. It is also a violation if an agency transfers funds from one program account to another without approval from Congress. (It should be noted that getting congressional approval to transfer funds is a lengthy process that may not be successful.)

The Time Limitation

Time is the second limitation with which agencies must comply. Most appropriated funds are available for a limited time, often called the *period of availability*, and they must be obligated within the period specified in the appropriations act, or they will expire. Any remaining balance is considered to be *expired funds*, unless it was obligated before the end of the period of availability. For example, if funds were appropriated for a one-year period, the agency must obligate the funds for the supplies or services within that one-year period of availability. The obligated funds are available beyond the one-year period so that payments can be made for expenditures made within that one-year period.

By placing time limits on the availability of appropriated funds, Congress maintains control and gives itself the right to review federal agencies' funding activities. The right of Congress to limit the expenditure and obligation of federal appropriations to specific time periods is supported by the statute at 31 USC 1502(a), which reads:

> The balance of an appropriation or fund limited for obligation to a definite period is available only for payment of expenses properly incurred during the period of availability or to complete contracts properly made within that period of availability and obligated consistent with section 1501 of this title. However, the appropriation or fund is not available for expenditure for a period beyond the period otherwise authorized by law.

This statute applies to fixed-term appropriations that are available only for payment of expenses "properly incurred" during the appropriation's period of availability and to complete contracts "properly made" during that period. Thus, if an agency has a genuine need for certain supplies or services but does not obligate the funds before the end of the appropriation's period of availability, the funds are no longer available to fill that need.

The limitation on the use of appropriated funds for particular times and objects goes back to an 1870 decision by attorney general Amos T. Akerman, (13 Op. Att'y Gen. 288, 292), who wrote:

> Congress has the right to limit its appropriations to particular times as well as to particular objects, and when it has clearly done so, its will expressed in the law should be implicitly followed. This view will not forbid the use in the next year of balances remaining from such appropriations at the end of this year in the payment of expenses incurred and contracts made within this year, as authorized in section 5 [of the Appropriations Act of July 27, 1870].

The Amount Limitation

The third limitation agencies must respect is the amount limitation. An agency may not overobligate or overspend its appropriation, or it will be in violation of the Antideficiency Act (31 USC 1341). The Antideficiency Act prohibits government employees from making payments or committing to make payments in the future for the acquisition of supplies and services unless there is a sufficient amount of appropriated funds in the agency's budget to cover the costs in full.

Depending on the severity of the violation, employees who violate the Antideficiency Act may be suspended from work without pay, removed from office, fined not more than $5,000, imprisoned for not more than two years, or both fined and imprisoned.

Of the three limitation elements, only the amount limitation is subject to the Antideficiency Act. Employees of the federal government, whether the executive, judicial, or legislative branch, would be in violation of the Antideficiency Act if they obligated funds or made payment for supplies or services in excess of funds available in their agency's budget. For example, a violation occurred when an employee made a $200,000 payment on an invoice from the agency's operation and maintenance (O&M) funds but only $198,000 was available.

The Antideficiency Act is applicable not only to employees of the executive, judicial, and legislative branches but also to wholly owned government corporations that receive appropriated funds and use them to operate.

THE BONA FIDE NEEDS RULE

The bona fide needs rule is one of the fundamental principles of appropriations law. It states that a fiscal year appropriation may be obligated only to meet a legitimate or bona fide need arising in, or continuing to exist in, the fiscal year for which the appropriation was made. In other words, funds may be obligated only to meet a legitimate need, and obligations must be made during the period of availability so that expenses can be charged to that period. The bona fide needs rule applies to the obligation of funds from annual and multiyear appropriations but does not apply to no-year appropriations.

The bona fide needs rule has a statutory origin and is codified at 31 USC 1502(a). What constitutes a bona fide need depends on the facts and circumstances surrounding each acquisition. However, for obligation purposes, there must be a legitimate need for the supplies or services during the period the funds are available.

The Applicability of the Bona Fide Needs Rule to Annual Appropriations

Agencies are authorized to obligate or expend their annual appropriations only for bona fide needs in the fiscal year specified in the appropriations acts. For example, the appropriation for a certain agency's O&M activities is available for a one-year period. To obligate these funds for supplies or services, the agency must have a bona fide need for the supplies or services during that one-year period. If the funds are obligated within the one-year period, they will remain available for new obligations or payments of invoices for all supplies or services acquired during that period.

The Applicability of the Bona Fide Needs Rule to Multiyear Appropriations

Based on past Government Accountability Office (GAO) decisions, the bona fide needs rule applies to multiple-year appropriations (Comp. Gen. B-232024, Jan. 4, 1989; Comp. Gen. B-235678, July 30, 1990). Multiyear appropriations may be used for bona fide needs arising at any time during the period the funds are available. Although the funds can be used to acquire supplies or services at any time during the period of availability, the bona fide needs rule for the last year of the appropriation applies in the same way as the bona fide needs rule for annual appropriations. For example, if an agency obligates funds from its three-year appropriations in the last month of the third year, it must ensure that the obligation satisfies a bona fide need for the third year and not the following year.

Continuing Needs under Multiyear Appropriations

A need that arises in one fiscal year and continues to exist in the following year may be a bona fide need for both fiscal years. If the agency does not obligate the funds in the first year even though the need exists at the time, and the need extends into the next fiscal year, it is chargeable to the second year's funds, not the first year's (B-197274, September 23, 1983). For example, if the boiler in a high-rise office building must be repaired to operate more efficiently, but it is not repaired until the second year funds are available, the obligation is properly chargeable to the second-year funding.

The Applicability of the Bona Fide Needs Rule to No-Year Appropriations

No-year funds have no fiscal year limitations and are available until expended. In 1965, GAO determined that the bona fide needs rule did not apply to no-year appropriations (43 Comp. Gen. 657 and 661, 1964). Federal agencies have an advantage under no-year appropriations because they have the flexibility to use their appropriations when they need the funds most. Congress, however, is at a disadvantage under no-year appropriations because it has no control over the funds from year to year.

Even though GAO determined that the bona fide needs rule does not apply to no-year appropriations, care should still be taken when obligating and expending taxpayer dollars.

The Applicability of the Bona Fide Needs Rule to Supply Contracts

A 1901 comptroller general decision (8 Comp. Gen. 346 and 348) reads:

> An appropriation should not be used for the purchase of an article not necessary for the use of a fiscal year in which ordered merely in order to use up such appropriation. This would be a plain violation of the law.

Based on this decision, an agency would be in violation of the bona fide needs rule if it obligated funds for supplies at the end of a fiscal year, but it did not need those supplies until the next fiscal year.

Consumable supplies ordered through supply contracts must fill a bona fide need, whether they are to be used immediately or gradually over a period of time. In a 1921 decision, the comptroller general made a distinction between consumable supplies used gradually over time and those that can be used immediately (1 Comp. Gen. 115). In this case, an agency placed an order for gasoline three days before the end of the fiscal year. The gasoline was to be delivered in monthly installments in fiscal year 1922. The comptroller general determined that because the contract for the gasoline purchase was awarded near the end of the fiscal year, the gasoline, as a consumable supply item, could not have been purchased to meet a need for fiscal 1921. Delivery would have been impossible before the start of the new fiscal year.

Based on this decision, agencies must obligate funds that are current and available in the fiscal year in which the consumable supplies are to be used in order to fulfill the bona fide needs rule. On occasion, agencies will order consumable supplies in one fiscal year and receive them in the next fiscal year. For this to be legal, the order must represent a legitimate bona fide need in the year it was ordered, and the delayed delivery must be beyond the agency's control.

Agencies may order supplies in one fiscal year even if they will not be used until the next fiscal year, but only for the purpose of maintaining a certain level of necessary supplies. Agencies must ensure that they are not stockpiling supplies that exceed their normal supply level.

The Applicability of the Bona Fide Needs Rule to Service Contracts

As a general rule, service contracts, like supply contracts, must address a bona fide need for the fiscal year in which the services are provided (B-277165, January 10, 2000). Service contracts can be severable or nonseverable. The general rule mandating that service contracts fulfill a bona fide need for the fiscal year in which the services are provided does not apply to nonseverable service contracts.

Severable Service Contracts

Severable service contracts can be separated into components and can meet separate needs of the government. To determine whether a service contract is severable or nonseverable, one must analyze the statement of work carefully. The type of contract may sometimes help determine whether a service contract is severable or nonseverable, but it should not be used as the only determining factor. Questions that may be helpful in determining whether a service contract is severable include:

- ◆ What kind of service is being provided?

- ◆ What is the nature of the work?

- ◆ Is the objective or goal expressed in definitive terms?

- ◆ Are there options in the contract?

- ◆ Does the contract have incremental elements of performance (e.g., a contract with tasks divided into components such as research, development, testing, and evaluation)?

- ◆ Does each incremental element result in a benefit?

- ◆ Is the work based on tasks or time?

- ◆ When will the work be completed?

Janitorial and lawn maintenance service contracts for recurring and continuing services are examples of severable contracts. These services are time based, and the government will receive some value on a daily basis. Contracts for management services and clerical services also provide recurring services that often extend into the next fiscal year. These are also considered to be severable. The portion of the contract that extends into the next fiscal year is chargeable to the funds that were obligated in the year the funds were available.

In general, severable service contracts must fulfill bona fide needs for the fiscal year in which the services are performed. Until recently, severable service contracts could not cross fiscal years, but two new statutes for both civilian (41 USC 2531) and military (10 USC 2401) agencies authorize agencies to enter into service contracts that cross fiscal years. The period of performance may not exceed 12 months.

Nonseverable Service Contracts

A nonseverable service contract produces a single outcome. It may not be divided into components, and it may not meet separate needs in different fiscal years. Nonseverable contracts may not cross fiscal years. Therefore, funds for these types of contracts must be obligated at the time the contract is awarded and must cover the entire period of performance.

An example of a nonseverable service contract is a firm fixed-price contract for a research study that requires a final report of the findings. The research study may not be divided into components, and the government receives nothing of value until it receives the final report. The final report is the single outcome.

Contracts for training courses also are considered to be nonseverable and may be funded in full even if the services extend into the next fiscal year. For example, agencies may fully fund training contracts that cover a two-year period as long as there is a legitimate need. Federal agencies may also obligate funds from prior-year appropriations for training courses that begin shortly after the beginning of the next fiscal year if the scheduling of the courses is beyond their control. This can be done only if the time elapsed between the award of the contract and the performance start date is not excessive (B-238940, February 25, 1991).

CHAPTER 2

Independent Government Cost Estimates

(FAR 4.803, 13.106-3, 15.404-1 and 406-1, 36.203, 36.605)

A *cost estimate* is the estimated cost or price of supplies or services to be purchased for the federal government. Commonly referred to as *independent government cost estimates* (IGCE) within the federal government, cost estimates are important in the acquisition process, but they are often prepared incorrectly. Acquisition audit reviews have shown that too many contracts have incomplete or inadequate estimates.

Sadly, some believe that government estimates are not important. Not long ago, an acquisition instructor noted that government estimates were not worth the paper they were written on, implying that they were not necessary. On the contrary: Cost estimates are essential. When a cost estimate is prepared properly and includes supporting information, it will help determine whether prices offered by vendors are fair and reasonable. Incomplete estimates or those that lack cost details make cost or price analysis much more difficult. All acquisition professionals should understand why cost estimates are important and how to develop and use them.

Cost estimates have three primary purposes. They are used:

♦ To reserve funds for the contract during the acquisition planning phase

- As a basis of comparison for costs or prices proposed by prospective vendors

- To determine price reasonableness if only one vendor responds to a solicitation.

COST ESTIMATES FOR CONTRACTS

The Federal Acquisition Regulation (FAR) does not require the government to prepare a cost estimate for each acquisition. When a cost estimate is prepared, it must be included in the contract file as documentation. (Documentation of all actions undertaken during the preaward phase should be placed in the contract file.)

Estimates for Contracts and Option Periods

Cost estimates should be prepared for all new contracts, delivery and task orders, and any modification that results in a monetary change to the contract. The estimate should represent the maximum probable cost for the supplies or services being procured.

Many agencies have acquisition policies that require the preparation of an estimate for acquisitions over the simplified acquisition threshold of $150,000. Some agencies also require cost estimates for complex acquisitions under the simplified acquisition method of contracting. Because the cost estimate is used to evaluate vendors' pricing during the evaluation phase of an acquisition, it is very important that it be kept in the contract file for reference.

A new cost estimate is not necessary if the government issues a contract modification to exercise a priced option period containing negotiated costs that have already been determined to be fair and reasonable. An *option period* gives the government a unilateral right to purchase additional supplies or services beyond the initial contract performance period or to extend the contract. A *priced option period* is an option period that has been evaluated; the specific amount of the option is specified in the contract. Option periods may include priced or unpriced supplies or services. An unpriced option lists the supplies or services to be provided in the contract but does not identify the price of the option. The option price is negotiated at the time the option is exercised.

Estimates for Commercial Items

It is not necessary to develop cost estimates for commercial items that are considered standard material, such as office supplies or printing services. Catalog or market survey prices may be used as an estimate for materials that are readily available and can be immediately purchased off-the-shelf in the commercial marketplace.

The Party Responsible for Estimates

The requesting office (often called the *program office*) is responsible for preparing the cost estimate for a proposed acquisition. Sometimes the contracting officer is called upon to help the program office prepare the estimate. The program office develops an estimate it considers reasonable and in line with current prices in the commercial marketplace. Cost is considered reasonable if a prudent businessperson would spend as much for the item or service, which is determined by reviewing historical data from private businesses/industry.

A cost estimate developed by the program office is usually based on current, reliable information, but sometimes estimates are "guesstimates" or are based on outdated information. A rough estimate might not be a very reliable price evaluation tool. Therefore, it is very important for the contracting officer to know where the information was obtained and to understand the pricing tools used to develop the cost estimate. Whoever prepares government cost estimates must have some experience or training in cost estimating.

Estimate Confidentiality

An IGCE is confidential. Under no circumstances should it be given to proposing vendors prior to receipt of proposals. It is also not wise to make it available to anyone outside the acquisition team that is preparing the preaward documentation for the proposed acquisition. This will prevent sensitive or proprietary information from being leaked to other agency employees and to people in the commercial marketplace. If sensitive or proprietary information is leaked to the commercial marketplace, the contracting officer may cancel the proposed acquisition if he or she determines that all vendors cannot compete equally.

TYPES OF COST ESTIMATES

The government normally uses two basic estimating methods when developing the IGCE: the lump sum estimate and the detailed estimate. When developing an IGCE, the program office reviews and considers many types of data. These include published prices from the commercial marketplace and price information from previous acquisitions. When using price information from previous acquisition actions, the information should be no more than two years old, because prices change rapidly in the commercial marketplace.

Lump Sum Estimates

A *lump sum estimate* projects the cost of an acquisition on a gross or bottom-line basis. This type of estimate is useful when the final award price can be determined without examining individual cost elements and fee or profit. Lump sum estimating can be used when the proposed acquisition is carried out under the full and open competition method of contracting, when purchasing commercial items, and for small-dollar and noncomplex projects. This is because a small, simple project usually has a well-defined scope of work with a low risk of unforeseen conditions and will not require any changes to the work for the total duration of the contract period. The type of work activity, not the cost, determines whether a project is simple. Acquisition of lawn maintenance is one example of a simple project.

Exhibit 2-1 shows a sample format for a lump sum estimate. This is only one of many formats used by various organizations. When used, it should be modified to fit the appropriate acquisition action.

EXHIBIT 2-1: Sample Lump Sum Cost Estimate				
Item name	Cost classification	Unit quantity	Unit measure	Cost estimate
Services to include mowing and trimming existing turf and blowing all hard surfaces for the months of April through November. Services not to exceed 28 mowing visits.	Lawn maintenance	1.0	Lump sum	$550.00
Fertilization services for existing turf in the months of March, May, July, September, and November. One application per month.	Lawn maintenance	1.0	Lump sum	$240.00
Edging of all sidewalks, curb line, and other applicable hard surfaces in every other mowing visit.	Lawn maintenance	1.0	Lump sum	$100.00
Trimming services for all ornamental grass and shrubs in November.	Miscellaneous	1.0	Lump sum	$100.00
Total cost estimate				$990.00

Detailed Estimates

A *detailed estimate* involves an analysis of the individual cost elements that are directly related to the requirements specified in the solicitation. The person responsible for preparing the estimate must have a good understanding of the government's requirements. The estimate should cover the entire performance period, including option periods, but can be done for only a portion of the proposed contract period if warranted. For example, if a contract has one base year and four option periods, the estimator may analyze only the base year.

When performing a detailed estimate, the following elements, at a minimum, must be analyzed:

- ◆ Direct labor

- ◆ Materials, if included

- ◆ Overhead amount or rates identified in percentages

- ◆ Other direct costs

- ◆ Amount of profit, in dollar amount or percentage.

A detailed estimate will help an agency:

- ◆ Determine the type of contract to be used

- ◆ Evaluate proposals received from competing vendors

- ◆ Develop negotiation positions that result in fair and reasonable prices that are acceptable to the federal agency and to the vendors who are awarded the contract.

The government and the contractor do not usually negotiate each cost element. These negotiations of cost elements are not necessary as long as the cost agreed upon is considered fair and reasonable.

Because an estimate is prepared in the early stages of the acquisition process, it is at times necessary to update the government's estimate before receiving proposals from competing vendors. Updating the detailed cost estimate is necessary if the consumer price index changes or changes are made to the requirements between the time the solicitation was issued and when proposals are received. If the requirements are changed during this time period, the solicitation must be amended and issued again to all interested parties.

See Exhibit 2-2 for a sample detailed cost estimate. The sample should be modified to fit the appropriate type of acquisition action. This is only one of many versions used within the federal government.

EXHIBIT 2-2: Sample Detailed Cost Estimate

Direct labor by category	Person days		Rate	Total
_____	_____	X	_____ =	_____
_____	_____	X	_____ =	_____
			Subtotal	_____

Fringe benefits (_____% of labor; leave blank if fringe benefits
are included in the direct labor category above)
Overhead (___% of labor and fringe benefits)   _____

Direct material costs
a. Purchased parts and supplies   _____
b. Subcontracts   _____
c. Other materials   _____

Total material costs   Subtotal _____
Other direct costs
a. Travel   _____
b. Consultants   _____
c. Other   _____
Total other direct costs   Subtotal _____

TOTAL DIRECT COSTS   _____

General and administrative expense
(_____%) × TOTAL DIRECT COSTS   _____
                                                      Subtotal _____
Fee* or profit**   _____

TOTAL ESTIMATED COSTS   _____

*The projected profit for cost-reimbursement contracts is called *fee*.
**The term *profit* (not fee) is used for fixed-price contracts.
The standard fee ranges from 5 percent to 15 percent, depending on the type of
contract, but may start below 5 percent. Percentages listed below are statutory
limitations (FAR 15.404-4(b)(4)(i)):
  • Research and development: not to exceed 15 percent of contract's estimated cost
  • Architect-engineer contract: not to exceed 6 percent of the estimated cost of
    construction.
  • Other cost-plus-fixed fee contracts: not to exceed 10 percent of the contract's
    estimated cost.

CHAPTER 3

Justifying Contract Awards without Full and Open Competition

(FAR 6.3)

Did you know that a written justification is required when an agency decides to award a contract without full and open competition and that the justification is required by law to be made available for public inspection? This written justification must be prepared in accordance with FAR 6.3 (Other than Full and Open Competition).

A recent acquisition audit reported that an agency had awarded a contract valued at $100 million to one vendor without the required justification and agency approvals for a noncompetitive solicitation. When written justifications are provided, audit review reports often find that they are inadequate, incomplete, and not prepared in accordance with FAR policy.

Preparation of a proper and complete justification always prevents contract problems. Acquisition professionals are strongly encouraged to comply with the statutory authority in FAR 6.3 when contracting without allowing for full and open competition.

EXEMPTION FROM FULL AND OPEN COMPETITION

The Competition in Contracting Act of 1984, as amended, mandates that all agencies use full and open competition for both the sealed bid and competitive negotiation methods of contracting unless exempted. Two statutory authorities allow federal agencies to execute contracts without using competitive procedures: 10 USC 2304(c) and 41 USC 253(c), as implemented in FAR 6.3. The Department of Defense (DoD), U.S. Coast Guard, and National Aeronautics and Space Administration (NASA) must comply with the provisions in 10 USC 2304(c); civilian agencies are subject to the provisions in 41 USC 253(c).

WRITTEN JUSTIFICATION FOR USING NONCOMPETITIVE PROCEDURES

The government must fulfill a series of requirements to justify and authorize the use of noncompetitive procedures. The justification to use noncompetitive procedures must comply with the policies and procedures in FAR 6.3. As required by FAR 6.301, when using other than full and open competition, agencies must solicit offers from as many potential vendors as practicable.

When a federal agency decides to award a contract without performing full and open competition or with limited competition, the contracting office must prepare a written justification. The justification should be reviewed by the agency's legal counsel for legal sufficiency and must be approved by the appropriate acquisition official. Most agency policies require the justification to be approved by the head of the contracting activity or the agency procurement executive when the acquisition is for a large-dollar, complex contract. Unless agency regulation or policy requires otherwise, many federal contracting officers have the authority to approve noncompetitive acquisition actions at or below a threshold of $550,000.

Sometimes, a program office will ask to purchase supplies or services without competition because its appropriated funds are about to expire. The impending expiration of an appropriation should never be used to justify using other than full and open competition. Requests for supplies or services must be made to fulfill a bona fide need, not just to expend funds before they expire. It is essential, then, that all requests for sole source acquisitions be reviewed carefully, particularly at the end of the fiscal year when funds are ready to expire.

Lack of advance acquisition planning sometimes leads program offices to request that supplies or services be procured from one vendor. Failure to plan ahead also may not be used to justify sole source acquisitions. All agencies are required to develop annual acquisition plans for all proposed acquisitions so that adequate funds are committed and the agencies' needs are met in a timely manner at reasonable cost.

Federal agencies can use various formats when writing the required justification for using other than full and open competition. Exhibit 3-1 shows a sample justification for using noncompetitive procedures for supplies or services. The sample can be modified to fit a particular requirement for any acquisition action for which full and open competition is not required. The sample includes all the justification line items that are identified in FAR 6.303-2 (Content).

EXHIBIT 3-1: Sample Justification for Other than Full and Open Competition

With *(name of vendor)*
Name of project _____ or contract number _____

1. Identification of the agency
Insert the following paragraph: The *(name of office)*, acting through the Department of *(name of agency)*, located in *(insert location)* purposes to *(identify work to be performed)* with *(name of company)*.

2. Nature and description of the action being approved
Insert the following paragraph: The *(name of office)* is seeking approval for a sole source procurement for *(identify the supplies or services)*.

3. Description of the supplies or services to be acquired and the estimated costs
Describe the supplies or services, including the total cost and the location where they are to be provided. The paragraph should be brief but comprehensive.

EXHIBIT 3-1: Sample Justification for Other than Full and Open Competition (cont.)

---

4. Identification of the statutory authority permitting other than full and open competition
Insert the following paragraph: The statutory negotiation authority for the sole source procurement is 41 USC 253(c)(1) or 10 USC 2304 (c)(1) implemented by FAR 6.302-1: Only one responsible source and no other supplies or services will satisfy agency requirements.

5. Demonstration of the proposed contractor's unique qualifications for the nature of the acquisition
Describe the qualifications of the vendor and why the vendor is the only one that can perform the work or provide the supplies.

6. Description of the efforts made to ensure that offers are solicited from as many potential sources as is practicable
Describe sources solicited, or insert the following sentence (if applicable): Not applicable to this procurement.

7. Determination by the contracting officer that the anticipated costs to the government will be fair and reasonable
Provide brief statement on costs, such as The contracting officer has determined that the anticipated cost to the government is fair and reasonable.

8. Description of the market survey conducted and the results or a statement of reasons a market survey was not conducted

9. Other facts supporting the use of other than full and open competition
Briefly discuss any additional reasons why sole source procurement is necessary for this effort.

10. Listing of sources, if any, that have expressed in writing any interest in this acquisition
Provide names of companies contacted, or insert the following if no vendors were contacted: No other sources were contacted.

11. Listing of the actions that the agency or organization will take to promote competition for any subsequent acquisitions for similar supplies or services required
Briefly explain why this acquisition will be competed in the future or why it cannot be competed in the future.

> **EXHIBIT 3-1:** Sample Justification for Other than Full and Open Competition (cont.)
>
> **CERTIFICATIONS**
>
> I certify that this justification is accurate and contains complete data necessary to support the recommendation for other than full and open competition.
>
> _____   _____
> Signature of contracting officer's   Date
> representative or designated program official
>
> I certify that this submission is accurate and that it contains complete information necessary to enable other officials to make an informed recommendation of approval or disapproval.
>
> _____   _____
> Signature of contracting officer   Date
>
> **APPROVED BY**
>
> _____   _____
> Signature of procurement executive   Date
> or head of the contracting activity

EXCEPTIONS FOR USING NONCOMPETITIVE PROCEDURES

The statutes exempting agencies from using competitive procedures do not define the term "other than competitive procedures." However, they do list seven exceptions for using other than full and open competition. These seven exceptions, listed below, permit agencies to purchase supplies or services with limited competition or on a sole source basis.

♦ **Exception 1:** There is only one responsible source, and no other supplies or services will satisfy agency requirements. FAR 6.302-1; 10 USC 2304(c)(1) or 41 USC 253(c)(1).

- ◆ **Exception 2:** The need for supplies or services is of unusual and compelling urgency. FAR 6.302-2; 10 USC 2304(c)(2) or 41 USC 253(c)(2).

- ◆ **Exception 3:** To achieve industrial mobilization; establish or maintain an engineering, developmental, or research capability; or acquire expert services. FAR 6.302-3; 10 USC 2304(c) (3) or 41 USC 253(c)(3).

- ◆ **Exception 4:** International agreement. FAR 6.302-4; 10 USC 2304(c)(4) or 41 USC 253(c)(4).

- ◆ **Exception 5:** Sole source acquisition is authorized or required by statute. FAR 6.302-5; 10 USC 2304(c)(5) or 41 USC 253(c)(5).

- ◆ **Exception 6:** National security. FAR 6.302-6; 10 USC 2304(c) (6) or 41 USC 253(c)(6).

- ◆ **Exception 7:** Public interest. FAR 6.302-7; 10 USC 2304(c)(7) or 41 USC 253(c)(7).

Contracting officers may award contracts without providing full and open competition or full and open competition after exclusion of sources when circumstances permit the use one of these seven statutory authorities. Each of these statutory exceptions contains applications and limitations for using other than full and open competition. Exceptions 1 through 6 require a written justification, and exception 7 requires a written *determination and findings*, a special form of written approval that is required before certain contracting actions may be taken when using noncompetitive procedures.

Publicizing the Intent to Award to One Source

Agencies are not required to request offers from as many potential sources as possible under exception 1. Exception 1 does not require civilian agencies to use the full and open competition method of contracting when the needed supplies or services can be obtained from only one responsible source that will satisfy their requirements. However, for DoD, NASA, and the Coast Guard, full and open competition does not have to be provided when the supplies or services are available from only one vendor or a limited number of vendors.

Although exception 1 permits using one responsible source, some degree of competition must still be considered. "Some degree of competition" means that agencies must publicize their intent to make an award on a sole source basis for all proposed acquisitions over $25,000. (The threshold can be less than $25,000 if the acquisition is considered to be advantageous to the government.) Any sealed bids or proposals for contracting by negotiation that are received in response to the sole source advertisement must be considered for contract award.

Requesting Offers from All Potential Vendors

The FAR specifically states that agencies must request offers from as many potential vendors as practicable for exceptions 2 (unusual and compelling urgency) and 6 (national security). But the requirement to solicit as many vendors as practicable is not limited to exceptions 2 and 6. The requirement also applies to exceptions 3 (industrial mobilization; engineering, developmental, or research capability; or expert services), 4 (international agreement), 5 (authorized or required by statute), and 7 (public interest).

BID PROTEST FORUMS AND THE USE OF NONCOMPETITIVE PROCEDURES

A written justification for the use of other than full and open competition that has been approved for any of the seven exceptions does not necessarily permit an agency to award a contract on a sole source basis. And there is no guarantee that the justification will hold up under the tight scrutiny of bid protest forums if a protest is filed.

Disgruntled vendors can use three protest forums in response to noncompetitive procedures:

- ◆ An agency-level bid protest
- ◆ The Government Accountability Office (GAO)
- ◆ The United States Court of Federal Claims.

Protests may be filed directly with an agency or GAO. The traditional forum for bid protest hearings is GAO, where most protests are filed. In recent years, it has become more common for vendors to bring bid protest actions before the Court of Federal Claims. The right for interested parties to file bid protests with the Court of Federal Claims is granted by 28 USC 1491(b)(1), which states:

> (b)(1) Both the [United] States Court of Federal Claims and the district courts of the United States shall have jurisdiction to render judgment on an action by an interested party objecting to a solicitation by a Federal agency for bids or proposals for a proposed contract or to a proposed award or the award of a contract or any alleged violation of statute or regulation in connection with a procurement or a proposed procurement. Both the United States Court of Federal Claims and the district courts of the United States shall have jurisdiction to entertain such an action without regard to whether suit is instituted before or after the contract is awarded.

Although this statute states that the district courts have jurisdiction to entertain protests, their jurisdiction expired on January 1, 2001, because Congress did not extend it (P.L. 104-320, section 12(d)).

A BID PROTEST CASE AND THE COURT OF FEDERAL CLAIMS DECISION

The following bid protest case illustrates why it is important to comply with the policies and procedures outlined by the FAR when justifying the use of noncompetitive procedures.

Savantage Financial Services, Inc., filed a protest with the Court of Federal Claims on January 11, 2008 (*Savantage Financial Services, Inc., v. the United States*, COFC No. 08-21C, April 15, 2008). Savantage was contesting the use of a brand name justification and improper sole source acquisition by the Department of Homeland Security.

Homeland Security, created in 2003 by merging 22 separate federal agencies, currently uses five different financial management operating systems. When the agency decided to integrate these five operating systems, the contracting officer prepared and signed a brand name justification on July 26, 2007. The justification identified the Oracle Corporation and SAP as the two financial management systems that would be used as the baseline for the integration of the five financial management operating systems. These two systems were part of the five financial management systems being used by Homeland Security.

A solicitation was issued in August 2007 for the integration process but was cancelled on October 4, 2007, because no proposals were received. On November 20, 2007, Homeland Security issued a task order under an existing contract to Oracle Corporation and SAP to provide support for the integration of the operating systems.

Savantage filed a protest requesting that Homeland Security be prohibited from proceeding with the integration initiative until it complied with all applicable statutory and regulatory requirements for the selection of a financial management operating system. Savantage contended that Homeland Security had violated the Competition in Contracting Act by using a brand name justification, thereby avoiding the use of full and open competition for the integration effort. It also contended that the selection process was arbitrary, capricious, and an abuse of discretion.

Upon review, the Court of Federal Claims agreed that the sole source decision to award contracts to Oracle Corporation and SAP was arbitrary and capricious. The court further agreed that there was abuse of discretion on the part of the contracting officer and that the decision violated acquisition law. On April 15, 2008, the Court of Federal Claims enjoined Homeland Security from proceeding with the acquisition until the agency conducted full and open competition in accordance with the statutory and regulatory requirements for the selection of an appropriate financial management operating system.

We see, then, that preparing and signing a justification to use a brand-name product or one particular vendor did not authorize the agency to exempt itself from using full and open competitive procedures.

Past bid protest data indicate that potential contractors protest sole source awards more frequently than they do the other exceptions in FAR 6.3. The data also show that some of the protests were sustained because the sole source justifications were not properly documented or authorized by appropriate agency officials. Some of the reasons GAO sustained these protests were that the federal agency in question:

- ◆ Failed to consider an incumbent contractor

- ◆ Excluded nonlocal companies that expressed interest

- ◆ Eliminated a vendor from consideration because the company's telephone number was missing from its file

- ◆ Took action that did not permit some degree of competition even though circumstances allowed it.

CHAPTER 4

Market Research

(FAR part 10)

Market research is the process of gathering, recording, and analyzing information about vendors and commercial products in the commercial marketplace. Correctly done, market research provides information on the range of commercial supplies or services available. It also helps determine whether full and open competition for an acquisition is feasible.

Federal agencies often overlook market research when developing contracts. Acquisition audit reports have found that market research documentation is not always included in contract files and that market research is infrequently performed for acquisitions made through interagency contracting.

Market research is a basic contracting fundamental. It must be performed for all acquisition actions over $150,000 unless the contract is to be awarded on a sole source basis. Although market research is not mandatory for actions under $150,000, it is in the best interest of acquisition professionals to perform some research for all competitive acquisition actions under that threshold. Information on just about any product used by the public is readily available online.

THE REQUIREMENT TO PERFORM MARKET RESEARCH

Three statutes require agencies to perform market research: 41 USC 253a(a)(1), 41 USC 264b, and 10 USC 2377. The requirement is implemented in FAR 10.001. The FAR policy states that agencies must conduct market research as appropriate before:

◆ Developing new requirements

◆ Soliciting offers for acquisitions in excess of $150,000

◆ Soliciting offers for acquisitions less than $150,000, if adequate information is not available and the cost of market research can be justified

◆ Soliciting offers for acquisitions that could lead to bundled contracts.

Conducting market research helps agencies find the most suitable approach to acquiring needed supplies and services. The Competition in Contracting Act at 41 USC 253a(a)(1)(B) requires federal agencies to use advance procurement planning and market research during the planning stage for the acquisition of supplies and services. Performing market research in the early stages of an acquisition action will, in most cases, help an agency identify qualified vendors that provide acceptable supplies and services that meet its needs. It helps agencies make good, sound business decisions.

FAR 2.101(b)(2) defines market research as "collecting and analyzing information about capabilities within the market to satisfy agency needs." A 1995 comptroller general decision (B-258713 and B-258714, February 13, 1995) explains what market research entails:

> A market survey is an attempt to ascertain whether other qualified sources capable of satisfying the government's requirements exist and may be informal, i.e., phone calls to federal or non-federal experts, or formal, i.e., sources-sought announcements in the CBD or solicitations for information or planning purposes.

CBD, as mentioned in the comptroller's decision, stands for *Commerce Business Daily*, a daily publication formerly issued by the Department of Commerce on federal acquisition opportunities that is no longer used by the federal government. Federal agencies were asked to stop using it in January 2002. Its replacement is the Federal Business Opportunities website, an electronic portal known as Fed-BizOpps (www.fbo.gov). The government uses this publicly accessible site to publish acquisition opportunities greater than $25,000 and to seek sources.

THE PARTY RESPONSIBLE FOR MARKET RESEARCH

It is the responsibility of the acquisition organization to perform market research before soliciting bids or proposals that are in excess of the simplified acquisition threshold of $150,000. Market research can also be performed for acquisitions that are under the simplified acquisition threshold when limited or inadequate information is available, as long as the cost of the research does not exceed the benefit.

Although market research is primarily the responsibility of the acquisition office that will develop the proposed contract, the program office that is requesting the needed supplies or services also plays a major role in this area. The program office is responsible for providing information on the government's requirements in writing and in sufficient detail to the acquisition office. Performing the market research based on the government's requirements will help the responsible acquisition office collect the appropriate data.

When requirements are sufficiently specific, the acquisition office can conduct adequate market research that will help it determine whether commercial or noncommercial supplies or services are available to meet the needs of the government. Market research can also help locate vendors that have the supplies or capability to provide the services needed by the government.

Adequate market research cannot be performed unless the requirements of the government have been well defined by the program office. Poorly defined requirements will lead to incomplete market research, which may lead to weak competition or an absence of competition. Inadequate market research can also lead to protests from vendors, which sometimes result in the cancellation of necessary contracts. Therefore, it is very important for program offices or other responsible government entities to develop well-defined requirements before the acquisition office conducts market research and completes other preaward acquisition documentation.

Market research based on well-defined requirements can also help justify using noncompetitive procedures. If market research justifies using other than full and open competition, the procedures at FAR 6.303-2 must be followed (see Chapter 3 for more information).

TYPES OF MARKET RESEARCH

Once the agency's needs are sufficiently defined, the acquisition office can conduct market research. Program offices sometimes compile a list of vendors that they believe are capable of providing the supplies or services they need. It is sometimes necessary for the acquisition office to do further research on these vendors to make sure they are still in business and are actually capable of providing the right type of supplies or services needed by the government.

Market research to identify potential vendors can be formal or informal. Formal market research techniques include publicizing the solicitation or making a formal announcement on FedBizOpps or performing market research online. Informal market research often involves contacting vendors that have already done business with the government and have a proven track record. Informal techniques that can be used to identify potential vendors include:

- ◆ Speaking by phone with federal or nonfederal experts or representatives of institutions of higher learning, manufacturing companies, and nonfederal organizations.

- ◆ Speaking by phone with acquisition personnel at other federal agencies.

- ◆ Reviewing market research data from contracts that are no more than five years old.

- ◆ Browsing catalogs or literature for supplies or services provided by vendors, manufacturers, and other marketing companies.

Regardless of the method used to conduct the research, the data gathered must be included in the contract file as reference material, as required by FAR 4.803 (Contents of Contract Files).

REQUESTS FOR INFORMATION FOR PLANNING PURPOSES

Federal agencies are allowed to issue solicitations for the purpose of obtaining acquisition information from the commercial marketplace or for identifying vendor capabilities when planning an acquisition strategy. FAR 15.201(e) permits the use of requests for information (RFIs) as follows:

> RFIs may be used when the Government does not presently intend to award a contract, but wants to obtain price, delivery, other market information, or capabilities for planning purposes. Responses to these notices are not offers and cannot be accepted by the Government to form a binding contract. There is no required format for RFIs.

Agencies can attract potential vendors by issuing a "sources sought" announcement on the FedBizOpps website. FAR 5.205(a) permits agencies to issue notices, referred to as *research and development advance notices*, seeking potential vendors for research and development projects when market research does not yield an adequate number of vendors for full and open competition. These types of notices cannot be used when security considerations prohibit publication. Because the FAR does not specifically state that advance notices publicized in FedBizOpps are limited to research and development acquisitions, many agencies issue advance notices for all types of acquisitions.

Market research data gathered from an RFI will help determine whether there are vendors in the marketplace with the expertise to meet the government's requirements. It will also help determine whether commercial or nondevelopmental items are available in the marketplace to meet the government's needs. *Commercial items* include supplies and services that are customarily used by the public or private enterprises and can in almost all cases be purchased off the shelf. *Nondevelopmental items* do not include prototype or experimental items. They do include:

- ◆ Items previously developed exclusively for the use of local, state, federal governments or their foreign allies

- ◆ Previously developed items that require only minor modification to meet the needs of the government

- ◆ Fully developed items currently in production but not yet sold or in use.

CHAPTER 5

The Statement of Work

(FAR 2.1, 8.405-2, 11.002, 15/2-4-1 and 2, 16.504, 35.005, 36.601-3)

The Services Acquisition Reform Act (SARA) of 2003 established an advisory panel to come up with recommendations for improving federal acquisition practices. The Acquisition Advisory Panel found that the federal government was not developing well-defined requirements. The private commercial sector did a better job defining its requirements because commercial organizations invested the necessary time and resources for requirements definition. Based on its review, the panel concluded that commercial organizations were able to get quality supplies and services at reduced prices because they had well-defined requirements and used full and open competition. The panel came up with 89 recommendations for improving federal acquisition practices. One of the recommendations called for federal agencies to improve their requirements definition. It is important for acquisition professionals to ensure that the government's requirements are well defined before soliciting offers from vendors.

THE PURPOSE OF A STATEMENT OF WORK

A *statement of work (SOW)* describes in detail the federal government's work requirements for projects that call for services to be performed or for the delivery of supplies. The SOW is the most important component of the acquisition process. It is the foundation of the contract and is used as a standard to measure the contractor's performance. The vendor must follow the SOW and may not deviate from it.

THE PREPARATION AND CONTENT OF THE STATEMENT OF WORK

Because the SOW is used to evaluate proposals and, eventually, contractor performance, it is a key element in any solicitation and must be prepared with great care.

The Party Responsible for the SOW

It is the responsibility of the agency program office to draft an SOW that defines the government's requirements in clear and definitive terms. The contracting officer, at the request of the program office, may help develop SOWs for more complex and high-dollar acquisitions. The contracting officer is responsible for reviewing and editing the SOW, if necessary, to ensure that the language is clear and that the SOW contains no outdated information. Any major changes to an SOW must be coordinated with the program office and approved by a designated approving official before the solicitation is released.

Specifications for Solicitations

The statutes at 41 USC 253a (a) (2) and 10 USC 2305 (a) (1) (B) mandate that every solicitation contain specifications that permit full and open competition:

> (2) Each solicitation under this subchapter shall include specifications which—
> (A) consistent with the provisions of this subchapter, permit full and open competition;
> (B) include restrictive provisions or conditions only to the extent necessary to satisfy the needs of the executive agency or as authorized by law.

The term *specifications*, as used in these statutes, refers to the work descriptions—now commonly called SOWs—that federal agencies must prepare. Although the terms *SOW* and *specification* are often used interchangeably, they are *not* one and the same. A specification is a type of standard that provides the essential details of the government's requirements and is normally attached to a contract or solicitation document. Specifications normally describe qualitative and quantitative design and performance requirements. These are usually referenced in the SOW, but the SOW rarely contains the complete details of specifications.

The SOW is the foundation of all contracts. Therefore, it must clearly define the work that must be done to produce or provide the supplies to be delivered or the services to be performed for the government. It must communicate explicitly and completely to the contractor what must be accomplished before the contractor is paid for delivery of the supplies or services.

In case of a dispute between the government and contractor, the courts often decide in favor of the contractor when the contract language is found to be ambiguous. In general, ambiguities are almost always interpreted against the drafter. The SOW does not have to be as detailed as a technical specification, but it must be well written so that it clearly:

♦ Permits full and open competition

♦ Reflects the needs of the government

♦ Reflects what is available in the open market

♦ Does not include restrictive provisions, unless permitted by law or the government requires special and unique supplies or services

♦ Encourages vendors to compete equally for contracts that are solicited by the government.

The Format of an SOW and Common Elements

The format and content of an SOW vary from agency to agency because they are dictated by the requirements of the government. For example, SOWs for the Department of Defense or the National Aeronautics and Space Administration quite often include many detailed tasks and subtasks or phases and subphases for their high-dollar and highly technical requirements.

The words and sentences used in an SOW should be simple and precise so that the government and industry personnel providing the needed supplies or services can understand the document. Regardless of their size or technical complexity, all SOWs share some common content elements:

- ◆ **Background.** A quick overview of the acquisition. Background information normally includes a general description of the requirements and the reason for the acquisition action, as well as citations of any statutory authorities that apply to the requirements.

- ◆ **Scope of work.** This section should outline what the SOW covers. It should contain a brief, general description of the supplies or services to be provided, the office or organization that will use the supplies or services, and a short explanation of why the acquisition is necessary. The information in this section should not be detailed; the details belong in the requirements section.

- ◆ **Documentation.** All the documentation that is required for the acquisition, such as specifications, standards, and other reference material associated with the requirements, should appear in this section. These documents in their entirety may be included as attachments to the SOW. If the documents are not included for security reasons or because there are too many documents to make inclusion practical, this section should state where the documents can be found.

- ◆ **Requirements.** This is the main body of the SOW. It contains explicit, detailed information on the work to be performed. The content of this section will be dictated by the requirements of the government. It may list many detailed tasks and subtasks. Any special requirements, such as security issues, a need for government-furnished property, and other requirements essential to meeting the needs of the government, should be included in this section. For very large and technically complex requirements, it is appropriate to include the delivery schedule and to state where the work is to be performed and the period of performance.

SOWs for Federal Supply Schedules

When an agency acquires certain supplies and services, such as installation, maintenance, and repair, from the Federal Supply Schedule Program, an SOW is not required, but the ordering procedures in FAR 8.405-1 must be followed. If an SOW is required when ordering from the Federal Supply Schedule Program, it must include the following information:

- ◆ The type of work to be performed

- ◆ The location where the work is to be performed

- ◆ The period of performance

- ◆ A description of the deliverable and the associated delivery schedule

- ◆ The performance standards by which the contractor is to be evaluated

- ◆ Any special requirements applicable to the order.

WHEN IS A STATEMENT OF WORK REQUIRED?

Most federal acquisitions require a comprehensive SOW. SOWs must be prepared:

- ◆ For all acquisitions that will use the negotiated method of contracting

- ◆ When acquiring the following services:

  - › Commercial and noncommercial work

  - › Research and development studies

  - › Consulting work

- ◆ When the simplified acquisition procedures are used to procure services

- ◆ For service acquisitions under the micropurchase threshold of $3,000

- ◆ For construction of at least or in excess of $2,000 subject to the Davis-Bacon Act

- ◆ For service acquisitions of at least or in excess of $2,500 subject to the Service Contact Act.

Acquisitions for supplies, especially commercial items, usually require only a description of the supplies, not a full SOW. Very technical, complex supply-acquisition projects sometimes require SOWs. Agencies sometimes find it necessary to write SOWs for medical, scientific, and technical equipment and supplies.

TYPES OF STATEMENTS OF WORK

SOWs can state specifications in terms of function, performance, or design. Acquisition regulations do not mandate the type of SOW to be used, so agencies have full discretion in selecting the kind that best meets their needs for each acquisition. The statutes at 41 USC 253a(a)(3) and 10 USC 2305(a)(1)(C) define each type of SOW:

> [The] type of specification included in a solicitation shall depend on the nature of the needs of the executive agency and the market available to satisfy such needs. Subject to such needs, specifications may be stated in terms of—

(A) function, so that a variety of products or services may qualify;
(B) performance, including specifications of the range of acceptable characteristics or of the minimum acceptable standards; or
(C) design requirements.

FAR 11.002(a)(2)(i) also offers acquisition personnel guidance on how to describe the government's requirements:

(i) State requirements with respect to an acquisition of supplies or services in terms of—
(A) Functions to be performed;
(B) Performance required; or
(C) Essential physical characteristics.

Sometimes, it is necessary to combine a functional or performance SOW with a design SOW to fully address essential details of the requirements. Highly technical and complex contracts quite often require a combination of two types of SOWs to adequately describe all the technical details.

The Functional-Based SOW

A *functional-based SOW* describes the "what, when, and where" of the supplies or services to be provided, and it allows the vendor the freedom to determine the most efficient means of accomplishing the work. The functional-based SOW is the most in-depth of the three types of SOWs. Most functional-based SOWs provide a generalized description of what is to accomplished based on the government's needs rather than on the way the work is to be performed.

Exhibit 5-1, a sample functional SOW for services, includes some of the standard essential elements of an SOW. This sample SOW is only one of many versions used by federal agencies.

EXHIBIT 5-1: Sample Functional SOW for Services

1. Background
Give a general but brief description of the requirement, explain why the acquisition is necessary, and cite the relevant statutory authority, if appropriate.

2. Scope of work
Example language: This statement of work covers project management, personnel, guard posts and schedules, duties and responsibilities of the guards, and agency post orders. This requirement is for the operation and management of guard services to prevent unauthorized access, maintain order, protect life, and prevent damage to government property.

3. Documents
Attach agency post orders to the statement of work, or provide information on where they can be found.

4. Work requirements
The need for guard services dictates the requirements (tasks) listed below. Each requirement should be explained clearly and in detail. If necessary, the tasks may be expanded to include subtasks.

4.1. Project management
Describe how the project is to be managed.

4.2. Personnel
Provide information on the types of personnel required for the contract.

4.3. Guard posts and schedules
Provide information on the location of posts to be guarded, including the clock times guard services must be provided.

4.4. Duties and responsibilities
Provide a detailed list of the guards' duties and responsibilities.

The Performance-Based SOW

A *performance-based SOW* describes the government's top-level objectives for an acquisition and is more appropriate for service contracts. It does not describe how the work is to be accomplished, but it does describe in detail the purpose of the work and the desired work output. A performance-based SOW gives proposing vendors the flexibility to be creative in their approaches. For example, most vendors respond to a performance-based SOW by describing what services they will provide, how they will provide them, and how their performance will be measured. The vendors provide standards for measuring their performance only if requested by the government. The winning vendor is expected to use the approach it outlined.

The Design-Based SOW

Statements of work that define design requirements or essential physical characteristics are used mostly for architect-engineer, construction, and commercial contracts. These statements describe in detail how the work is to be performed and materials are to be used. For example, a construction SOW will describe the nature and volume of work as well as the estimated price range of the project. (The government's independent cost estimate for the project should never be revealed, but an estimated cost, stated as a range, may be included.) Usually, when acquiring commercial items, it is necessary to describe their essential physical characteristics so that vendors can provide the items that will best meet the needs of the government.

CHAPTER 6

Acquisition Methods and Selecting the Appropriate Type of Contract

(FAR parts 14, 15, and 16)

In the past few years, acquisition audit reviews have found that there is a growing trend toward the use of time-and-materials and cost-plus contracts. Unfortunately, these contract types are often selected only because the government cannot explain what it wants. They place little risk on the contractor and are very costly, practically allowing the contractor to spend as much as it wants to, so they should not be used unless their use can be justified. Acquisition professionals should spend taxpayer dollars wisely by making an effort to use contract types that impose sufficient but not undue risk on the contractor to encourage good performance.

TWO BASIC ACQUISITION METHODS

There are two basic methods of contracting within the federal government: sealed bidding and contracting by negotiation. One of these two methods must be used for all noncommercial acquisitions exceeding the simplified acquisition threshold of $150,000. The contracting officer, in coordination with the program office requesting the supplies or services, is responsible for deciding which method will be used. Their decision is based on the SOW, which dictates the method and type to be used.

Because the SOW dictates which method and type of contract will be used, it is extremely important that the requirements specified in the SOW be clearly defined.

FAR part 6 requires the government to promote full and open competition (unless exempted pursuant to FAR 6.3) when acquiring supplies or services. One of the following methods must be used for both sealed bidding and contracting by negotiation:

- ◆ Full and open competition
- ◆ Full and open competition after exclusion of sources
- ◆ Other than full and open competition.

Sealed Bidding

The sealed bidding method of contracting has been used by the federal government since 1809. This method is used when the government's requirements can be described accurately and completely in clear language, without any ambiguities. It is a competitive process in which bids are solicited though an invitation for bids (IFB). The invitation is sent to prospective bidders or published on the FedBizOpps website, www.fbo.gov.

This method was referred to as *formal advertising* when the winning vendor was selected on the basis of price only. It was the preferred method until 1984, when the Competition in Contracting Act allowed both the sealed bidding and competitive negotiation methods to meet the competition requirements, thereby reducing the use of sealed bidding. Federal agencies now use competitive negotiation more often than sealed bidding.

The statutory policies and procedures for sealed bidding are provided in 41 USC 253(a)(b) and 10 USC 2305(a)(2)(B) and implemented in FAR part 14 (Sealed Bidding). The statutory requirements for opening of bids and award and notification to competing vendors are provided in 41 USC 253b(c) and 10 USC 2305(b)(3) as follows:

> Sealed bids shall be opened publicly at the time and place stated in the solicitation. The executive agency shall evaluate the bids in accordance with subsection (a) of this section without discussions with the bidders and, except as provided in subsection (b) of this section, shall award a contract with reasonable promptness to the responsible source whose bid conforms to the solicitation and is most advantageous to the United States, considering only price and the other price-related factors included in the solicitation. The award of a contract shall be made by transmitting, in writing or by electronic means, notice of the award to the successful bidder. Within 3 days after the date of contract award, the executive agency shall notify, in writing or by electronic means, each bidder not awarded the contract that the contract has been awarded.

Conditions for Sealed Bidding

The sealed bidding method may be used when all of the following conditions can be met:

◆ There is sufficient time to prepare the solicitation.

◆ There is sufficient time for interested bidders to submit sealed bids.

◆ There is sufficient time for the government to evaluate the sealed bids.

◆ The award can be made based only on price and price-related factors.

◆ The government's requirements are clear and definitive and do not require discussions with the bidders.

◆ The government expects, based on market research, to receive more than one sealed bid.

FAR 14.104 requires the government to use a fixed-price contract or, if authorized, a fixed-price contract with economic adjustments when the sealed bidding contracting method is chosen.

Forms Used for Sealed Bidding

Except for construction and architect-engineering services, FAR 53.214 requires that the following forms be used for the solicitation of sealed bids and award of the contract:

- Standard Form (SF) 26, *Award/Contract*, is used for award when SF-33, *Solicitation, Offer and Award*, is used to solicit bids.

- SF-30, *Amendment of Solicitation/Modification*, is used when amending IFBs.

- SF-33, *Solicitation, Offer and Award*, is used to solicit bids as well as to award the contract resulting from the bids. (This form is the one most commonly used by federal agencies and appears as Exhibit 6-1.)

- SF-1447, *Solicitation/Contract*, is used to award a contract resulting from sealed bidding and may be used in place of SF-26 or SF-33.

- SF-1409, *Abstract of Offers*, and SF-1410, *Continuation*, are used for recording bids received from vendors.

Opening Sealed Bids

Proposing vendors are required to seal their bids before submitting them to the government. These bids are opened by contracting officers in a public place that is usually identified in the IFB. Opening the bids in a public place is key: It protects the government and bidding vendors from fraud or favoritism and assures all parties that the award is made in accordance with the specifications stated in the invitation.

EXHIBIT 6-1: Standard Form 33 (Solicitation, Offer, and Award)

SOLICITATION, OFFER AND AWARD	1. THIS CONTRACT IS A RATED ORDER UNDER DPAS (15 CFR 700)	▶	RATING	PAGE	OF	PAGES

2. CONTRACT NUMBER	3. SOLICITATION NUMBER	4. TYPE OF SOLICITATION	5. DATE ISSUED	6. REQUISITION/PURCHASE NUMBER
		☐ SEALED BID (IFB) ☐ NEGOTIATED (RFP)		

7. ISSUED BY	CODE	8. ADDRESS OFFER TO (If other than Item 7)

NOTE: In sealed bid solicitations "offer" and "offeror" mean "bid" and "bidder".

SOLICITATION

9. Sealed offers in original and _____ copies for furnishing the supplies or services in the Schedule will be received at the place specified in Item 8, or if handcarried, in the depository located in _____ until _____ local time _____

(Hour)   (Date)

CAUTION - LATE Submissions, Modifications, and Withdrawals: See Section L, Provision No. 52.214-7 or 52.215-1. All offers are subject to all terms and conditions contained in this solicitation.

10. FOR INFORMATION CALL:	A. NAME	B. TELEPHONE (NO COLLECT CALLS)		C. E-MAIL ADDRESS
		AREA CODE	NUMBER	EXT.	

11. TABLE OF CONTENTS

(X)	SEC.	DESCRIPTION	PAGE(S)	(X)	SEC.	DESCRIPTION	PAGE(S)
		PART I - THE SCHEDULE				PART II - CONTRACT CLAUSES	
	A	SOLICITATION/CONTRACT FORM			I	CONTRACT CLAUSES	
	B	SUPPLIES OR SERVICES AND PRICES/COSTS				PART III - LIST OF DOCUMENTS, EXHIBITS AND OTHER ATTACH.	
	C	DESCRIPTION/SPECS./WORK STATEMENT			J	LIST OF ATTACHMENTS	
	D	PACKAGING AND MARKING				PART IV - REPRESENTATIONS AND INSTRUCTIONS	
	E	INSPECTION AND ACCEPTANCE			K	REPRESENTATIONS, CERTIFICATIONS AND OTHER STATEMENTS OF OFFERORS	
	F	DELIVERIES OR PERFORMANCE					
	G	CONTRACT ADMINISTRATION DATA			L	INSTRS., CONDS., AND NOTICES TO OFFERORS	
	H	SPECIAL CONTRACT REQUIREMENTS			M	EVALUATION FACTORS FOR AWARD	

OFFER (Must be fully completed by offeror)

NOTE: Item 12 does not apply if the solicitation includes the provisions at 52.214-16, Minimum Bid Acceptance Period.

12. In compliance with the above, the undersigned agrees, if this offer is accepted within _____ calendar days (60 calendar days unless a different period is inserted by the offeror) from the date for receipt of offers specified above, to furnish any or all items upon which prices are offered at the price set opposite each item, delivered at the designated point(s), within the time specified in the schedule.

13. DISCOUNT FOR PROMPT PAYMENT (See Section I, Clause No. 52.232-8)	10 CALENDAR DAYS (%)	20 CALENDAR DAYS (%)	30 CALENDAR DAYS (%)	CALENDAR DAYS (%)

14. ACKNOWLEDGMENT OF AMEND-MENTS (The offeror acknowledges receipt of amendments to the SOLICITATION for offerors and related documents numbered and dated):	AMENDMENT NO.	DATE	AMENDMENT NO.	DATE

15A. NAME AND ADDRESS OF OFFER-OR	CODE	FACILITY	16. NAME AND TITLE OF PERSON AUTHORIZED TO SIGN OFFER (Type or print)

15B. TELEPHONE NUMBER			15C. CHECK IF REMITTANCE ADDRESS IS DIFFERENT FROM ABOVE - ENTER SUCH ADDRESS IN SCHEDULE.	17. SIGNATURE	18. OFFER DATE
AREA CODE	NUMBER	EXT.	☐		

AWARD (To be completed by Government)

19. ACCEPTED AS TO ITEMS NUMBERED	20. AMOUNT	21. ACCOUNTING AND APPROPRIATION

22. AUTHORITY FOR USING OTHER THAN FULL AND OPEN COMPETITION:	23. SUBMIT INVOICES TO ADDRESS SHOWN IN (4 copies unless otherwise specified)	▶	ITEM
☐ 10 U.S.C. 2304(c) ( ) ☐ 41 U.S.C. 253(c) ( )			

24. ADMINISTERED BY (If other than Item 7)	CODE	25. PAYMENT WILL BE MADE BY	CODE

26. NAME OF CONTRACTING OFFICER (Type or print)	27. UNITED STATES OF AMERICA	28. AWARD DATE
	(Signature of Contracting Officer)	

IMPORTANT - Award will be made on this Form, or on Standard Form 26, or by other authorized official written notice.

AUTHORIZED FOR LOCAL REPRODUCTION
Previous edition is unusable

STANDARD FORM 33 (REV. 9-97)
Prescribed by GSA - FAR (48 CFR) 53.214(c)

Once all the bids have been opened, the contracting officer and the designated technical representative from the program office evaluate the bids. The evaluation is performed without discussion because the sealed bidding method does not permit any discussion between the government and vendors. The only communication that takes place between the government and proposing vendors is through the IFB and the written bids.

Awarding the Contract

Award must be made to a responsible vendor that submits the lowest bid considered to be advantageous to the government. The vendor's responsiveness is another very important element of the sealed bidding method; when a bid is considered nonresponsive, the government must reject it. A bid is considered responsive if it complies exactly with the requirements specified in the IFB.

Because discussions between vendors and the government are not permitted, the supplies or services provided by the vendor selected for award may be only minimally acceptable. Since weaknesses, deficiencies, and poor past performance cannot be discussed with sealed bidders, the government at times may not be able to obtain the best value for its money. The no-discussion policy could also lead to problems for the government later in the contract period. For example, the contractor might be consistently late in the delivery of the required services or supplies or might need guidance on a daily basis.

Two-Step Sealed Bids

In addition to the conventional sealed bidding method, there is a two-step sealed bidding process in which a combination of competitive procedures is used. This process is used when the government does not have adequate specifications. It is used mainly for the acquisition of complex items and requires the submission of technical proposals.

In the first step of this process, prospective vendors are asked to submit technical proposals only, which are evaluated and, if necessary, discussed with the vendors. The objective of this step is to determine whether the supplies or services proposed by the vendors would be acceptable.

Next, the vendors whose proposals were deemed acceptable are asked to submit sealed price bids. The processes used under the conventional sealed bidding method to receive and open price proposals are also used in the two-step sealed bidding process.

Finally, the government awards the contract to a responsible bidder whose bid complies with the technical requirements in the bid invitation. The bid selected is the one that is most advantageous to the government based only on the price and price-related factors specified in the invitation.

Contracting by Negotiation

The term *contracting by negotiation* refers to any type of acquisition that does not use sealed bidding. Negotiated contracts include both competitive and noncompetitive acquisitions and may be fixed-price or cost-reimbursement contracts.

The Armed Services Procurement Act of 1947 (10 USC 2302 et seq.), which was approved in February 1948, allowed the military agencies to use negotiation techniques as an alternative method of contracting. Civilian agencies were permitted to use the negotiated method of contracting upon implementation of the Federal Property and Administrative Services Act of 1949 (41 USC 251 et seq.). This statute requires that contracting by negotiation be used only if the sealed bidding method is found to be not feasible or practicable.

The decision to use negotiated acquisition procedures is within the discretion of the contracting officer. However, the contracting officer must reasonably conclude that the conditions that would allow for the use of the sealed bidding method are not present before using the negotiated method of contracting.

Contracting by negotiation is both a competitive and noncompetitive process in which vendors are required to submit both technical and price proposals. Contracting by sealed bidding emphasizes price factors alone, but when contracting by negotiation, the emphasis is on the technical aspects of the proposals. Cost or price factors are important when using the negotiated method, but their relative importance varies depending on the type of negotiated acquisition it is.

Contracting by negotiation gives federal agencies the flexibility to use various acquisition strategies and procedures. The negotiated method of contracting does not allow proposals to be opened in public, and discussions between the government and proposing vendors are permitted, per FAR 15.306(d):

> (d) Exchanges with offerors after establishment of the competitive range. Negotiations are exchanges, in either a competitive or sole source environment, between the Government and offerors, that are undertaken with the intent of allowing the offeror to revise its proposal. These negotiations may include bargaining. Bargaining includes persuasion, alteration of assumptions and positions, give-and-take, and may apply to price, schedule, technical requirements, type of contract, or other terms of a proposed contract. When negotiations are conducted in a competitive acquisition, they take place after establishment of the competitive range and are called discussions.

Discussions between the two parties often result in the government permitting the vendors to make changes to their proposals, but vendors are not allowed to completely revise their initial proposals.

Discussions are not mandatory when using negotiated procedures, but some vendors in the commercial marketplace expect to discuss negotiated acquisitions with the government. When discussions are not held, occasionally disgruntled vendors will protest, usually during the solicitation phase.

Conditions for Contracting by Negotiation

When one or more of the conditions allowing the use of the sealed bidding method cannot be met, contracting by negotiation must be used. Negotiated procedures are used when the following conditions are met:

◆ The government expects to receive more than one proposal.

◆ The government intends to award the contract based on non-price-related factors, such as technical or management factors.

◆ The government finds it necessary to hold discussions to ensure that the proposing vendor understands the needs of the government.

◆ The government has determined that a fixed-price contract is not appropriate and cannot be used for the acquisition.

Source Selection Processes and Techniques

Contracting by negotiation requires the government to design an acquisition strategy. The first step in this strategy is to devise the source selection approach that will be used to select the proposal with the best value and that is most advantageous to the government. The acquisition team develops the selection process before soliciting proposals.

The term *best value* has been around for years, but it was not used consistently until the 1990s. In a nutshell, the *best value* source is the one that will provide the greatest benefit to the government in response to its requirements. FAR 2.101 defines best value as "the expected outcome of an acquisition that, in the Government's estimation, provides the greatest overall benefit in response to the requirement."

Two source selection processes are used to ensure that the government gets the best value. The *lowest price technically acceptable source selection process* is used when the government expects to get the best value from the technically acceptable proposal with the lowest evaluated price. The government uses the *trade-off process* when the contract award is expected to be made to a vendor other than the one whose offer has the lowest price or highest technical rating.

All evaluation factors and subfactors contained in the acquisition strategy must be included in the solicitation issued to the public. However, the rating method to be used by the evaluation panel need not be disclosed to the public. The relative importance of the factors and subfactors must be stated in the solicitation. FAR 15.304(e) provides the following guidance on the importance of the evaluation factors and subfactors:

> (e) The solicitation shall also state, at a minimum, whether all evaluation factors other than cost or price, when combined, are—
> (1) Significantly more important than cost or price;
> (2) Approximately equal to cost or price; or
> (3) Significantly less important than cost or price (10 USC 2305(a) (3)(A)(iii) and 41 USC 253a(c)(1)(C).

The Lowest Price Technically Acceptable Process

The lowest price technically acceptable process has been used for many years and is considered a best value procedure. Under this process, the contract is awarded to the vendor that submits a technically acceptable proposal with the lowest evaluated price. The lowest price technically acceptable process is appropriate when there are minimal performance risks and the government's requirements are well defined. FAR 15.101-2 mandates the following when using the lowest price technically acceptable process:

♦ The solicitation must include the evaluation factors and significant subfactors that will be used to determine acceptability.

♦ The solicitation must specify that the contract will be awarded to the vendor whose proposal meets or exceeds the acceptability standards for non-cost factors and has the lowest evaluated price.

- Past performance of proposing vendors will not be evaluated if the agency contracting officer determines it is not appropriate and documents the reason it is not an appropriate evaluation factor.

- Past performance of proposing vendors will be evaluated if the agency contracting officer decides to use it as an evaluation factor.

- When the agency contracting officer determines that a small business's past performance is not acceptable, the business must be referred to the Small Business Administration for a certificate of competency determination.

- Cost and price trade-offs are not permitted under the lowest price technically acceptable process.

- Technical proposals are evaluated to determine acceptability but are not ranked when using non-cost or price factors or subfactors.

- Discussions may be held with vendors if the agency contracting officer deems them necessary.

This process appears similar to sealed bidding, but there is one major difference between the lowest price technically acceptable process and the sealed bidding method: The former allows discussions to be held with proposing vendors prior to selection of the proposal with the best value. Vendors who submit proposals that do not meet all the evaluation requirements may be given an opportunity to correct any deficiencies through discussions or in writing. Discussions and correction of deficiencies are appropriate only if the award will not be made based on vendors' initial proposals.

The use of the lowest price technically acceptable process has been protested on occasion by disgruntled vendors, who complain that the sealed bid method is more appropriate when price is the determining factor for the acquisition. However, the comptroller general has upheld the use of the negotiated method of contracting in many of these cases, particularly in those with very complex technical and management requirements, because in-depth discussion was necessary to determine the best value for the government.

The Trade-Off Process

The government uses the trade-off process when it believes that it can achieve best value by awarding the contract to a vendor other than the one whose proposal has the lowest price or the highest technical rating. Using the trade-off process gives the government the flexibility to trade off among cost or price and non-cost evaluation factors, such as the contractor's:

- ◆ Technical capabilities
- ◆ Management capabilities
- ◆ Qualifications
- ◆ Experience.

The trade-off process is appropriate if the government's requirements are complex, and the government is willing to pay extra for contractor capability and skills, reduced risk, and other non-cost factors because the extra benefits are worth the pay. A solicitation using the trade-off process normally states that award will be made to the vendor that submits the proposal that is deemed to represent the best value to the government. The determination of best value is based on three evaluation factors:

- ◆ Technical capability
- ◆ Past performance
- ◆ Price.

A written justification containing relevant facts and supporting rationale is required when the government selects a higher-priced proposal. The justification must explain why the higher-priced proposal was chosen and identify the benefits or advantages the government will receive for the added cost. A written justification is also required when the government determines that the non-cost benefits offered by a higher-priced but technically superior proposal are not worth the price.

When using the trade-off process, FAR 15.101-1 requires that the solicitation:

♦ Clearly state the evaluation factors and subfactors that will affect contract award

♦ Note the relative importance of these factors and subfactors

♦ State whether all non-cost or -price factors, when combined, are significantly more important than cost or price, of approximately equal importance to cost or price, or significantly less important than cost or price.

THE PROPOSAL EVALUATION PROCESS

The evaluation of proposals is performed by an evaluation panel, commonly referred to as the *technical evaluation panel* or *source selection evaluation board*. Depending on the complexity of the acquisition, the panel may consist of one person or as many as ten or more. As required by the FAR, the panel must be impartial while performing the evaluation.

When the evaluation process is complete, the contracting officer determines the competitive range and selects the vendors whose proposals scored in the competitive range for further consideration. The competitive range may include as few as three, four, or five top-scoring vendors. FAR 15.306(c)(1) and (d)(1) permit the government to limit the competitive range to only the "most highly rated proposals" and does not require that discussions be held with vendors that are not included in the competitive range.

Negotiations may be held with vendors in the competitive range if the contracting officer decides that they are necessary. When negotiations are held, vendors are advised by the contracting officer of any deficiencies in their proposals and are asked to submit revised proposals for further evaluation. An acquisition official called the *source selection authority* selects the proposal with the best value. It has been said by many acquisition experts that the source selection decision is subjective because the process gives the source selection authority very broad discretion in selecting the proposal with the best value. However, acquisition regulations require the source selection authority to use reasonable business judgment in the selection process. The source selection authority must justify his or her selection in writing.

Finally, the contracting officer awards the contract to the vendor whose proposal has been determined to be the best value to the government, price and other factors considered.

TYPES OF CONTRACTS

A wide selection of contract types may be used to acquire supplies and services for the federal government under the sealed bidding or contracting by negotiation methods. These contract types can be grouped into four broad categories: fixed-price, cost-reimbursement, indefinite-delivery, and other contract types (Exhibit 6-2). Different contract types may be used individually or in combination.

EXHIBIT 6-2: Types of Contracts			
Fixed-price (FAR 16.2)	Cost-reimbursement (FAR 16.3)	Indefinite-delivery (FAR 16.5)	Other contract types (FAR 16.6)
• Firm fixed-price • Fixed-price with economic price adjustment • Fixed-price incentive • Fixed-price with prospective price redetermination • Fixed-ceiling-price with retroactive price redetermination • Firm fixed-price, level-of-effort	• Cost • Cost-sharing • Cost-plus-incentive-fee • Cost-plus-award-fee • Cost-plus-fixed fee	• Definite-quantity • Requirement • Indefinite-quantity	• Time-and-materials • Labor-hour • Letter

Contracts that result from the sealed bidding method must be firm fixed-price or fixed-price with economic price adjustment, but any type of contract or combination of types may be used when contracting by negotiation. Selecting the appropriate type of contract for an acquisition is essential to its successful performance and completion.

Fixed-Price Contracts

Fixed-price contracts are suitable when acquiring supplies and services that can be described in sufficient detail and when price is agreed upon during the award phase. Under a fixed-price contract, most of the performance and cost risks are placed on the contractor. For example, the contractor will be paid the contract price agreed upon even if it costs the contractor more to complete the work. (Of course, if it costs the contractor less to complete the work, it will still be paid the amount originally agreed upon and will end up making more profit.)

Cost-Reimbursement Contracts

Cost-reimbursement contracts allow the government to pay the contractor all allowable costs that are reasonably incurred as prescribed in the contract. This type of contract is used when there are many uncertainties associated with contract performance and contract costs cannot be estimated with sufficient accuracy to use a fixed-price contract. A cost-reimbursement contract provides an estimate of the total costs for the purpose of obligating funds, and it establishes ceilings that may not be exceeded during the period of performance. Of the major types of contracts, cost-reimbursement contracts place the least cost and performance risk on the contractor. The contractor is just required to put forth its best effort to complete the work.

Indefinite-Delivery Contracts

Indefinite-delivery contracts for supplies do not specify the quantity to be purchased. In general, delivery or task orders are used for delivery of supplies or services under indefinite-delivery contracts. A delivery order is an order for supplies, and a task order is an order for services; both are placed against an existing contract.

Multiple awards can be made under indefinite-delivery contracts. The statute at 10 USC 2304c(b) and 41 USC 253j, implemented by FAR 16.505(b)(1), mandates that all contractors who win multiple-award contracts be given a fair opportunity to be considered for orders in excess of $3,000.

Vendors that believe the government breached the fair-opportunity provision in their contracts do not hesitate to file a bid protest or submit a claim for monetary compensation. For example, the Link Simulation & Training Division of L-3 Communications Corporation submitted a claim to the U.S. Air Force contracting officer on May 28, 2004, and subsequently to the Armed Services Board of Contract Appeals (ASBCA) alleging that the fair-opportunity provision in its contract was breached (ASBCA, No. 54920, May 8, 2008). Link claimed that the U.S. Air Force:

◆ Performed an improper price evaluation

◆ Did not consider Link's past performance to be of equal importance to the technical factors

◆ Performed a flawed and biased evaluation of its technical proposal.

The claim for the breach submitted by Link to the contracting officer was denied. Link appealed this decision to the ASBCA, which found that there was no breach of the fair-opportunity provision in the air force's evaluation of Link's technical proposal and past performance. However, the ASBCA found that the air force did breach the fair-opportunity provision by performing an improper price evaluation. Based on the findings, the ASBCA sustained the appeal on May 5, 2008, and determined that Link was entitled to recover $186,482 for its proposal preparation and submission costs in response to the U.S. Air Force's delivery order proposal.

Other Types of Contracts

Three types of contracts do not fall into the fixed-price, cost-reimbursement, or indefinite-delivery categories: Time-and-materials, labor-hour, and letter contracts.

Time-and-Materials and Labor-Hour Contracts

Time-and-materials and labor-hour contracts are appropriate when it is not possible to accurately estimate the extent or duration of the work to be performed to any reasonable degree. Time-and-materials contracts are used to purchase supplies or services based on the number of fixed direct labor hours the contractor spends performing the work, including materials at cost when applicable. Labor-hour contracts are similar to time-and-materials contracts but do not cover the cost of materials.

Time-and-materials and labor-hour contracts may be used only when the contracting officer determines that another type of contract is not suitable and justifies this determination in writing. Federal agencies are required to limit the use of time-and-materials and labor-hour contracts because of the risk they impose on the government. Most contractors do not have an incentive to control costs under time-and-materials and labor-hour contracts. Thus, ceiling prices are included in these contracts to control costs. Contractors assume the risk for exceeding ceilings.

Concerned about the use of time-and-materials contracts, Congress asked the Government Accountability Office (GAO) in fiscal year 2007 to perform an audit within the Department of Defense (*Defense Contracting: Improved Insight and Controls Needed over DoD's Time-and-Materials Contracts* (GAO-07-273, June 2007)). The audit team found that the defense agencies were turning to time-and-materials contracts because they could be awarded quickly. The team also found that contracting officers often did not justify in writing the decision to use a time-and-materials contract, contract monitoring was inconsistent, and few attempts were being made to convert follow-on work to a different type of contract.

Letter Contracts

A letter contract is a preliminary document, in the form of a letter, that permits contractors to begin performing work without a legally binding and enforceable contract. The government uses letter contracts infrequently.

A letter contract provides only a schedule for definitizing the contract. It includes three dates:

- The date the contractor is to submit its price proposal and any required make-or-buy program. *Make-or-buy* refers to a contractor's plan that identifies the major items it will produce or the work it will perform in its facilities (i.e., *make*) and the products or services the contractor will subcontract out to another vendor (i.e., *buy*).

- The date of the start of contract negotiations.

- The target date for definitizing the contract.

All the necessary contract terms and conditions must be negotiated within 180 days from the date a letter contract is issued or before 40 percent of the work is completed. In addition, unless approved in advance by an authorized government official, the cost of the definitized contract must not exceed 50 percent of the estimated cost of the letter contract. A letter contract may not be used unless the head of the contracting activity determines in writing that no other contract type is suitable. It should be used only if the need for the supplies or services is of an unusual and compelling urgency.

THE PROHIBITION OF COST-PLUS-A-PERCENTAGE-OF-COST CONTRACTS

A cost-plus-a-percentage-of-cost contract includes a specified fee or percentage of profit based on the actual cost to the vendor of performing the work. The federal government is prohibited from using this type of contract by two statutes: 41 USC 254(b) for civilian agencies and 10 USC 2306(a) for noncivilian agencies. The prohibition appears in FAR 16.102(c):

> The cost-plus-a-percentage-of-cost system of contracting shall not be used (see 10 U.S.C 2306(a) and 41 USC 254(b). Prime contracts (including letter contracts) other than firm-fixed-price contracts shall, by an appropriate clause, prohibit cost-plus-a-percentage-of-cost subcontracts (see clauses prescribed in Subpart 44.2 for cost-reimbursement contracts and Subparts 16.2 and 16.4 for fixed-price contracts).

This prohibition applies to both the sealed bidding and contracting by negotiation methods. Cost-plus-a-percentage-of-cost contracts offer no incentive to government contractors to minimize costs. Instead, they provide an incentive for contractors to increase costs to increase profit.

For example, when materials handling charges are included in the overhead hourly rate and are also listed as a separate contract cost under a time-and-materials contract, the contractor would be paid twice for materials handling. This would be a violation of the federal acquisition statute prohibiting cost-plus-a-percentage-of-cost contracts. FAR 16.6(c)(3) currently allows materials handling costs to be charged as a separate cost item under a time-and-materials contract as long as the cost is not included in the labor hourly rate.

In another example, a construction contractor entered into a contract that specified a percentage of profit—say 10 percent—beyond the actual cost of the construction project. If the construction project costs $20 million to complete, the contractor will receive $22 million for the work. There is little incentive for the contractor to hold down costs in this scenario. Another type of contract, such as a cost-plus-fixed-fee, would have been a better choice for the government because it would cost the government less.

To avoid violating the cost-plus-a-percentage-of-cost prohibition, it is essential to remove from a contract any provision that indicates that the contractor's compensation will be computed as a percentage of the cost of performance. However, there is no violation if the profit or fee provision in the contract allows for a fixed amount of compensation and clearly indicates that the compensation is not to be computed as a percentage of cost. Offering fixed rates for overhead, profit, fee, and labor costs also is allowed.

CHAPTER 7

Performance-Based Acquisition for Services

(FAR 2.1, 7.1, 12.1, 32.10, 37.101, and 103, 37.6)

In an effort to improve federal acquisition methods and procedures, in 2005 the Acquisition Advisory Panel reviewed seven parts of the federal acquisitions system. The panel found that there was a need for improvement in the implementation of performance-based acquisition (PBA). The Office of Federal Procurement Policy (OFPP) has encouraged greater use of performance-based contracting since 1991, but the panel found it had not been fully implemented by federal agencies. The panel reported that agencies were not clearly defining their requirements, developing adequate statements of work, identifying meaningful quality measures and effective incentives, or effectively managing contracts.

To improve their use of performance-based contracting, acquisition professionals must understand the processes that govern it, and they must help program offices develop clear performance requirements, measurable performance standards, and quality assurance plans.

PERFORMANCE-BASED ACQUISITION: BACKGROUND

Performance-based acquisition was established to allow the government to acquire services in a more cost-effective manner. It can:

- ◆ Save the government money
- ◆ Maximize contractor performance

- ◆ Reduce contractor performance risk

- ◆ Attract creative and innovative contractors

- ◆ Increase competition in terms of contractors and solutions

- ◆ Improve the level of services provided to the government.

One of two types of performance work statements must be used by federal agencies for a performance-based contract: a performance work statement or a statement of objectives.

In 1991, the OFPP, which is responsible for providing overall direction on federal acquisition policies, regulations, and procedures, issued Policy Letter 91-2 to all federal agencies. The letter stated that performance-based acquisition was the preferred method for services contracting. The policy was developed to ensure that vendors had the freedom and flexibility to decide how best to fulfill the government's needs. Policy Letter 91-2 has since been rescinded, but the policy itself became public law and was implemented by FAR part 37 (Services Contracting).

In 1994, OFPP initiated a pilot project to encourage the use of performance-based contracts for services. This pilot project covered services for building maintenance and security, information technology support, and aircraft and technical support. Since that time, performance-based contracting has helped some agencies save money and receive better-quality services.

Despite these successes, performance-based acquisition has not yet been fully implemented governmentwide. This is primarily due to personnel's lack of experience in writing performance-based statements of work. OFPP is still encouraging and working with agencies to develop policies and procedures for implementing performance-based service acquisition.

The Definition of Performance-Based Acquisition

Performance-based acquisition is defined in FAR 2.101 as follows: "Performance based acquisition (PBA) means an acquisition structured around the results to be achieved as opposed to the manner by which the work is to be performed." FAR 37.6 (Performance- Based Acquisition.) provides policies and procedures for the acquisition of services when using performance-based methods.

The Order of Precedence for Performance-Based Acquisition

Performance-based acquisition was established as the preferred method for the acquisition of services by P.L. 106-398, section 821, which was enacted on October 30, 2000. This law is implemented in FAR 37.102, which states that "performance-based acquisition is the preferred method when acquiring services." The method is to be used by federal agencies to the maximum extent practicable.

FAR 37.102(a)(2) establishes the following order of preference for contracts used to acquire services:

(i) A firm-fixed price performance-based contract or task order.

(ii) A performance-based contract or performance-based task order that is not firm-fixed price.

(iii) A contract or task order that is not performance-based.

THE PERFORMANCE WORK STATEMENT

The performance work statement (PWS) describes contract work in terms of the required outcome or results. It does not describe the manner in which the work is to be performed. A PWS is intended to allow vendors the freedom to be creative and innovative in determining how best to meet the government's objectives. Performance-based acquisitions are considered to be more cost-effective because government contractors are held accountable for the end results of the work.

A PWS is usually prepared by the government program office, but acquisition teams sometimes decide that it is in their best interest to ask proposing vendors to develop the statement. Vendors can often offer well-defined statements because they are well versed in the services they provide. FAR 37.602(b) states that agencies must, to the maximum extent practicable, do the following when developing a PWS:

> (1) Describe the work in terms of the required results rather than either "how" the work is to be accomplished or the number of hours to be provided (see 11.002(a)(2) and 11.101);
> (2) Enable assessment of work performance against measurable performance standards;
> (3) Rely on the use of measurable performance standards and financial incentives in a competitive environment to encourage competitors to develop and institute innovative and cost-effective methods of performing the work.

There is no preferred format for a PWS, but a good statement should include performance requirements, performance standards, and a quality assurance plan, which may include financial incentives. These elements encourage greater vendor competition, which leads to more cost-effective acquisitions. If any one of these elements is missing from the contract, the performance-based approach will not be successful. A performance-based contract that includes all three elements will prevent cost overruns, delivery delays, poor service, and other performance problems (e.g., reduced contractor accountability).

Performance Requirements

The performance requirements must be clearly written, so that the proposing vendors understand what is to be produced or performed. It is extremely important to remember that vendors should not be told *how* the work is to be accomplished, but rather what is to be achieved—the objectives of the acquisition. This gives vendors the flexibility to be creative and to find the best and most economical ways to do the work.

Performance Standards

Performance standards describe in measurable terms how good the contract work must be. They must be connected to the performance requirements. The government (or, in some cases, vendors) may set performance standards for quality, quantity, production level, delivery schedule, response time, and the number of customer complaints.

Financial incentives can be included in the performance standards as well, if necessary, to encourage the contractor to provide services that exceed a satisfactory rating. For a large, high-dollar acquisition, it is appropriate to include both negative and positive financial incentives. When a negative financial incentive has been set and performance is less than satisfactory, payment is reduced by a certain percentage.

The Development and Content of a Quality Assurance Plan

A quality assurance plan describes how the government will measure a contractor's performance against the performance standards included in the contract. The quality assurance plan must correspond to the performance standards so that it can measure whether the contractor is meeting all the requirements specified in the PWS. The plan must describe the method or methods that will be used to determine whether the performance standards have been met. For example, if the government wants to make unannounced periodic inspections, they must be mentioned in the plan.

Developing a quality assurance plan that describes the quality standards by which a performance-based contract will be measured and managed can be a complex process. This plan is just as important as the performance requirements or the government's objectives, and it is necessary in order to achieve the performance objectives negotiated between the government and contractor.

Before deciding how the performance of the contractor will be measured and managed, the quality standards that will be used must be identified. The government has three options for choosing the standards that will be included in a quality assurance plan:

◆ Developing the quality standards and associated quality assurance plan

◆ Using commercial quality standards, such as the standards developed by the International Standards Organization 9000

◆ Asking the proposing vendors to develop the standards and the quality assurance plan.

Developing a Quality Assurance Plan Using Commercial Quality Standards

Instead of developing new quality standards for new requirements that are highly complex and technical, the government sometimes finds that using commercial quality standards is the most feasible option. For example, the International Standards Organization (ISO) 9000 offers a family of standards for quality management that apply to all types of organizations, including information technology, government, manufacturing, servicing, electronics, legal services, accounting, construction, health care, aviation, and many others. Many private organizations in the United States and around the world use these standards because they provide reliable quality control, and using them is economical. A complete, up-to-date listing of the ISO standards can be found at http://www.iso.org/iso/iso_catalogue.htm.

Contractor-Prepared Quality Assurance Plans

For most contracts, the government prepares the performance standards and the associated quality assurance plan. However, the government sometimes asks vendors to prepare the quality assurance plan, especially for technically complex contracts. When vendors are asked to prepare the quality assurance plan, the solicitation must include a provision informing the vendors that they are to develop the quality assurance plan based on standards provided by the government. They must also be informed that the performance measures proposed may be changed, if necessary, during performance of the contract.

Audit reports issued by the Government Accountability Office within the last several years revealed that many performance-based contracts for services had cost overruns or schedule delays, and some did not meet the performance standards set by the federal government. Service contracts must have well-defined requirements that are linked to measurable performance standards to avoid cost overruns, schedule delays, and the delivery of unacceptable work. These contracts must also have good quality assurance plans along with good contract monitoring so that weaknesses and deficiencies in a contractor's performance are identified early.

THE STATEMENT OF OBJECTIVES

The statement of objectives (SOO) lists brief, overall performance objectives associated with the government's top-level requirements. FAR 2.1 defines the statement of objectives as follows:

> Statement of Objectives (SOO) means a Government-prepared document incorporated into the solicitation that states the overall performance objectives. It is used in solicitations when the Government intends to provide the maximum flexibility to each offeror to propose an innovative approach.

When the government decides to ask proposing vendors to develop innovative solutions for its requirements, it develops and issues an SOO with the solicitation. An SOO is normally used when there the government does not have enough information on the type of supplies or services it needs. The SOO describes the desired results of the acquisition in terms of objectives and how those objectives relate to the mission of the federal agency that developed it. The SOO is brief, so it does not fully describe the desired results.

Then, based on the SOO, the proposing vendors must develop solutions for the government's objectives. Because the vendors are guided only by overall performance objectives, they are free to devise an innovative approach to meeting the needs of the government. In short, instead of the government describing in detail the work to be accomplished, the vendors propose detailed options and solutions. These options and solutions become the government's PWS.

The SOO may not be made a part of the contract. It must be removed from the solicitation and replaced with the PWS prepared by the winning vendor upon award of the contract.

A hypothetical SOO for lawn maintenance services illustrates how the government might state its objectives. Instead of requiring the contractor to mow the lawn weekly, the SOO would indicate that the lawn must be kept between four and five inches high at all times and must be watered and fertilized when appropriate. Because the proposing vendors have expertise in lawn maintenance, they would be able to determine how and when the lawn would be maintained.

In another illustration, an existing building is being renovated, and a new generator is needed. The SOO for the project would describe the characteristics of the generator the government needs, but would allow the proposing vendors to suggest available generator models, for example. In both scenarios, the SOO transfers the responsibility for preparing the PWS from the government to the proposing vendors.

The Format and Content of an SOO

FAR 37.602(c) requires agencies to include, at a minimum, the following elements in an SOO:

- ◆ Purpose
- ◆ Scope or mission
- ◆ Period and place of performance
- ◆ Background

- ◆ Performance objectives (required results)

- ◆ Any operating constraints.

Only the necessary objectives, which will be included in the PWS, must be identified in the SOO. It cannot be emphasized enough that the SOO should be structured around the purpose of the work to be performed, not how the work is to be performed. Exhibit 7-1 shows a sample format for an SOO, based on the elements mandated by the FAR.

EXHIBIT 7-1: A Sample Statement of Objectives
(Based on FAR 37.602(c))

1. Purpose
State simply and succinctly what is being purchased.

2. Scope or mission
Briefly but thoroughly describe the necessary work tasks and desired end results, and explain how the requirements relate to the agency's program or mission.

3. Period and place of performance
Note the period of time over which the work is to be performed (e.g., one base year and four option years) and the location where the work is to be performed.

4. Background
Provide a brief overview of the government project or program sponsoring the project, and explain why the project is needed and how it will relate to previous, current, and future projects.

5. Performance objectives (required results)
Describe the work in clear, definitive terms, including the requirements that the finished product or services must fulfill in order to be considered acceptable to the government.

6. Operating constraints, if any
List and describe, when appropriate, constraining factors such as government security, privacy, safety, policies, and standards. Although the purpose of an SOO is to allow vendors flexibility and creativity, it is sometimes necessary to put constraints on their approach.

The Quality Assurance Plan When Using an SOO

When a solicitation uses an SOO, and the government wants vendors to develop the work performance standards and quality assurance plan, it must request this in the solicitation. In almost all cases, vendors' quality standards will meet the government's expectations. Using the SOO approach gives vendors the flexibility and freedom to develop performance standards in line with their own internal quality standards and business practices. The vendors can also easily describe how their performance should be monitored and their work results evaluated.

When choosing work performance standards, whether they are developed by the government, by vendors, or by the International Standards Organization, it is very important to select only essential standards that are connected directly to the objectives of the acquisition. Selecting too many standards to measure success may not be cost-effective and may reduce the value of services provided. And measuring performance by too many standards can be time consuming. For example, the contractor might spend so much time complying with standards, the quality of its services will diminish. It is important, then, to keep costs in mind so that the cost of measuring contractor performance does not exceed the cost of services provided.

CHAPTER 8

The Federal Small Business Program

(FAR part 19)

The small business program is probably the least understood component of the federal government acquisition system. The program, like the federal acquisition system, is governed by complex laws and regulations. Those responsible for the program are often not included in the planning stage of acquisition actions. There is seldom any coordination between acquisition professionals and small business professionals. When the groups do communicate, it usually happens late in the acquisition process and long after any meaningful input can be made by the small business professionals.

Currently, more and better coordination is needed between the small business and acquisition offices within every government agency. To ensure that they are afforded sufficient opportunities to participate in federal contracts, it is imperative that all acquisition professionals understand the contracting requirements that govern the small business program. The information provided in this chapter highlights some small business policies and procedures that will ensure fair awards to small businesses. It is recommended that small business professionals be made a part of the acquisition team during the planning stage of all new acquisition actions.

THE PURPOSE OF THE SMALL BUSINESS PROGRAM

The Small Business Preference Program was established to ensure that small companies received their fair share of contracts and sub-contracts for federal government supplies and services. It was also intended to allow small businesses to receive a fair share of property sold by the government and to maintain and strengthen the economy of the United States. Small businesses represent 99.7 percent of all companies in the United States; in 2006, there were 25.8 million small businesses in the United States. They make valuable contributions to our economy by creating jobs, developing American products and technologies, contributing a substantial amount of funds to our tax revenues, and encouraging free competition. They are the foundation of the U.S. economy.

SMALL BUSINESS CONCERNS AND FEDERAL ACQUISITIONS

The Small Business Act defines a *small business concern* as a business that "is independently owned and operated and which is not dominant in its field of operation." Federal agencies are responsible for developing and implementing policies that will help small business concerns get their fair share of federal contracts. Congress created the United States Small Business Administration (SBA) as an independent federal agency through the Small Business Act of July 30, 1953, to assist small businesses. The small business program was then established and implemented by SBA, as mandated by the Small Business Act. The policy for small business concerns, as declared by Congress, appears in 15 USC 631(a) (Declaration of Policy):

> a) Aid, counsel, assistance, etc., to small business concerns. . . . It is the declared policy of the Congress that the Government should aid, counsel, assist, and protect, insofar as is possible, the interests of small-business concerns in order to preserve free competitive enterprise, to insure that a fair proportion of the total purchases and contracts for property and services for the Government (including

but not limited to contracts for maintenance, repair, and construction) be placed with small business enterprises, to insure that a fair proportion of the total sales of Government property be made to such enterprises, and to maintain and strengthen the overall economy of the Nation.

The Competition in Contracting Act of 1984, legislated at 41 USC 252(b) (small business concerns; share of business), reiterates the congressional policy in a brief statement: "It is the declared policy of the Congress that a fair proportion of the total purchases and contracts for property and services for the Government shall be placed with small business concerns."

Congress authorized a number of programs to help small businesses navigate the federal acquisition system. Social and economic goals are the primary focus of these programs (i.e., using federal contracts to achieve national goals by promoting small and disadvantaged businesses) and are under the management and control of the SBA, which aids, counsels, assists, and protects the interests of small business concerns. In short, the SBA helps U.S. citizens start, build, and grow small businesses that help to maintain and strengthen the U.S. economy.

Small Business Size Standards

The Small Business Act required the SBA to establish size standards for small businesses. Small businesses are identified as such either by the number of people they employ or based on the company's average annual receipts. All federal agencies use SBA's size standards to determine if a business is eligible to compete for a contract that has been specifically designated for small businesses. To be eligible for participation in the federal government's small business program, a business may not exceed SBA's maximum size standards. SBA is not responsible for certifying business firms as small businesses, nor does it keep a listing of eligible small businesses. When a small business wants to be considered as a source for an acquisition, it is responsible for certifying that it meets the size standard identified in the solicitation or loan application.

SBA's size standards are all matched to the North American Industry Classification System (NAICS) and can be found on the SBA website at http://www.sba.gov/contractingopportunities/officials/size/GC-SMALL-BUS-SIZE-STANDARDS.html. The most common size standards identified by the SBA are as follows:

- ◆ 500 employees for most manufacturing and mining industries
- ◆ 100 employees for all wholesale trade industries
- ◆ $6.5 million for most retail and service industries
- ◆ $31 million for most general and heavy construction industries
- ◆ $750,000 for most agricultural industries.

Exhibit 8-1 shows a detailed partial table of SBA size standards. The size standards set the maximum number of employees a for-profit business may have, or the maximum annual receipts it may take in, and still qualify as a small business for federal programs—except for federal acquisitions. To participate in the federal acquisition program, a vendor must meet the small business size standard that the contracting officer specifies in the solicitation. The size standard specified by the contracting officer is from SBA's size standards.

When vendors intend to compete as prime contractors, they must register in the Central Contractor Registration database. This database identifies the types of contracts registered contractors may perform.

NAICS codes	NAICS U.S. industry title	Size standard (millions of dollars)	Size standard (number of employees)
EXHIBIT 8-1: Partial Table of Small Business Size Standards Matched to North American Industry Classification System (NAICS) Codes			
Sector 51: Information			
Subsector 517: Telecommunications			
517110	Wired telecommunications carriers		1,500
517210	Wireless telecommunications carriers (except satellite)		1,500
517410	Satellite telecommunications	$13.5	
517911	Telecommunications resellers		1,500
517919	All other telecommunications	$23	
Subsector 518: Data Processing, Hosting, and Related Services			
518210	Data processing, hosting, and related services	$23	
Subsector 519: Other Information Services			
519110	News syndicates	$6.5	
519120	Libraries and archives	$6.5	
519130	Internet publishing and broadcasting and web search portals		500
519190	All other information services	$6.5	
Sector 52: Finance and Insurance			
Subsector 522: Credit Intermediation and Related Activities			
522110	Commercial banking	$165 million in assets	
522120	Savings institutions	$165 million in assets	
522130	Credit unions	$165 million in assets	
522190	Other depository credit intermediation	$165 million in assets	
522210	Credit card issuing	$165 million in assets	
522220	Sales financing	$6.5	
522291	Consumer lending	$6.5	
522292	Real estate credit	$6.5	

The Certificate of Competency and Responsibility Requirements

A certificate of competency (COC) is a document issued by the SBA to a contracting officer when a small business is the apparent winner of a government contract but has been found to be nonresponsible by a government agency. The COC certifies that the small business is responsible and that it has the capability to perform work for a specific government contract. In addition to meeting the small-business size standard identified in the solicitation, a small business must also fulfill the responsibility requirements stated in FAR 19.601(b) to receive and perform government contracts. These elements of responsibility include, but are not limited to, capability, competency, capacity, credit, integrity, perseverance, and tenacity, as well as the business's adherence to limitations on subcontracting.

THE SMALL BUSINESS SET-ASIDE PROGRAM

The Small Business Preference Program, more commonly called the Small Business Set-Aside Program (SBSA), is one of the oldest programs set up to help small businesses. The program was established to make sure that small businesses receive a fair share of federal government contracts. This is done by reserving or setting aside certain acquisition activities specifically for small businesses. The agency contracting officer can unilaterally decide to make a small business set-aside, or this decision can be made jointly when a set-aside is requested by the SBA and agreed to by the contracting officer. Regulations, however, specify that to the extent practicable, contracting officers alone should determine when to make small business set-asides.

Before deciding to set aside an acquisition, the contracting officer must perform a market survey, review the acquisition history of the business, and seek advice from the agency's small business office.

Total and Partial Set-Asides for Small Businesses

As authorized by 15 USC 644 and implemented in FAR 19.5 (Set-Asides for Small Business), the government may establish total set-asides or partial set-asides.

Total set-asides are acquisitions that have been set aside strictly for small businesses to perform. *Partial set-asides* are portions of acquisitions reserved to be awarded to small businesses. The remaining balance of a partial set-aside may be awarded to any firm, regardless of size. The government does partial set-asides when it determines that a small business cannot provide all the required supplies or services. FAR 19.502-3 authorizes partial set-asides when it has been determined that:

> (1) A total set-aside is not appropriate (see 19.502-2);
> (2) The requirement is severable into two or more economic production runs or reasonable lots;
> (3) One or more small business concerns are expected to have the technical competence and productive capacity to satisfy the set-aside portion of the requirement at a fair market price;
> (4) The acquisition is not subject to simplified acquisition procedures.

However, FAR states that:

> (5) A partial set-aside shall not be made if there is a reasonable expectation that only two concerns (one large and one small) with capability will respond with offers unless authorized by the head of a contracting activity on a case-by-case basis. Similarly, a class of acquisitions, not including construction, may be partially set aside. Under certain specified conditions, partial set-asides may be used in conjunction with multiyear contracting procedures.

Acquisitions Exempt from Set-Asides for Small Businesses

Federal agencies are not required to set aside acquisitions below the micropurchase threshold of $3,000 (or $15,000 for contingency operations or defense-related activities and $25,000 for foreign purchases and work in foreign countries) or when purchasing from the federal government's mandatory sources of supply.

FAR 8.002 lists the mandatory federal government supply sources in order of priority:

> **(1) Supplies.**
> (i) Agency inventories;
> (ii) Excess from other agencies;
> (iii) Federal Prison Industries, Inc.;
> (iv) Supplies which are on the Procurement List maintained by the Committee for Purchase From People Who Are Blind or Severely Disabled;
> (v) Government wholesale supply sources;
> (vi) Mandatory Federal Supply Schedules;
> (vii) Optional use Federal Supply Schedules; and
> (viii) Commercial sources (including educational and nonprofit institutions).
> **(2) Services.**
> (i) Services which are on the Procurement List maintained by the Committee for Purchase From People Who Are Blind or Severely Disabled;
> (ii) Mandatory Federal Supply Schedules;
> (iii) Optional use Federal Supply Schedules; and
> (iv) Federal Prison Industries, Inc., or commercial sources (including educational and nonprofit institutions).

Small Businesses Eligible to Participate in Set-Asides

The government may set aside a contract for full and open competition among all eligible small businesses, or it may limit the competition to only one class of business. Small business concerns that are eligible to participate in the federal government's set-aside program include:

◆ Small businesses

◆ Veteran-owned small businesses

◆ Service-disabled veteran-owned small businesses

- ◆ Historically underutilized business zone (HUBZone) small businesses

- ◆ Small disadvantaged businesses

- ◆ Woman-owned small businesses.

Small Businesses

Small businesses are normally privately owned and operated corporations, partnerships, or sole proprietorships that are qualified as small businesses by SBA. These businesses, including their affiliates, are profit-making organizations with a small number of employees and a relatively low volume of sales. A small business must not be dominant in its field of operation on a national basis and must be qualified as a small business by SBA.

Veteran-Owned Small Businesses

A small business concern that is owned by one or more veterans— and ownership by the veteran(s) is not less than 51 percent—is defined as a *veteran-owned small business.* FAR 19.201 requires that veteran-owned small businesses and other small business concerns be given the maximum opportunities practicable to participate as contractors or subcontractors in contracts awarded by the federal government.

Service-Disabled Veteran-Owned Small Businesses

The Service-Disabled Veteran-Owned Small Business (SDVOSB) Program was created by the Veterans Benefits Act in 2003 to provide federal contracting assistance to service-disabled veteran-owned small businesses. The contracting officer can restrict competition to businesses under the SDVOSB program only if there is reasonable expectation that two or more service-disabled veteran-owned small business concerns will submit offers and that the award can be made at a fair and reasonable price.

HUBZone Businesses

The HUBZone program was created to provide contracting assistance to small businesses located in historically underutilized business zones in urban and rural areas. The primary purpose of the program is to stimulate economic development and create jobs.

Small Disadvantaged Businesses

The Small Disadvantaged Business Program was developed to help small business concerns that are owned and operated by socially and economically disadvantaged individuals to obtain government contracts. Businesses that qualify as small disadvantaged businesses are usually owned and operated by African Americans, Asian Americans, Hispanics, and Native Americans. Other ethnic groups may qualify, but only if they can show evidence that they are disadvantaged. To be eligible to perform contracts under this program, the business must meet the following criteria:

◆ It must qualify as a small business.

◆ At least 51 percent of the business must be owned and controlled by one or more individuals who are both U.S. citizens and socially and economically disadvantaged.

◆ The business must be certified by SBA as eligible to participate in the Small Disadvantaged Business Program.

The 8(a) Business Development Program was established in 1969 to help small disadvantaged businesses become self-sufficient and competitive. The name is derived from section 8(a) of the Small Business Act. Through this program, SBA enters into all types of contracts with other agencies and awards subcontracts to eligible firms, commonly called 8(a) contractors. SBA serves as the prime contractor for the agency that made the contract award to SBA, and the small disadvantaged business serves as the 8(a) subcontractor to SBA. Under this arrangement, the 8(a) subcontractor performs the contract work for the contract between SBA and the other agency. Contracts performed by 8(a) contractors may be on either a sole source or a competitive basis. Detailed information on the 8(a) program can be found in FAR 19.8 or on the SBA website at http://www.sba.gov/aboutsba/sbaprograms/8abd/.

Woman-Owned Small Businesses

To be identified as a woman-owned small business concern, at least 51 percent of a business must be owned, controlled, and operated by women who are U.S. citizens. As required by FAR 19.201, woman-owned small businesses and other small businesses must be given the maximum practicable opportunity to participate as either contractors or subcontractors in contracts awarded by the government. Woman-owned businesses as a group are not considered socially or economically disadvantaged. However, if a woman owner is socially or economically disadvantaged, the business may participate as a contractor or subcontractor in three business programs: small business, small disadvantaged business, and woman-owned small business.

DOLLAR THRESHOLDS RESERVED FOR SMALL BUSINESS CONCERNS

Government agencies are required to set aside acquisitions for competition among small businesses when the agency contracting officer determines that there is a reasonable expectation of receiving offers from two or more vendors. There are, however, certain dollar thresholds to which the contracting officer must adhere when reserving proposed contracts for small business concerns. FAR requires the acquisition methods and associated dollar thresholds described below to be reserved for small business concerns.

Micropurchases from Commercial Businesses

The acquisition of supplies or services that do not exceed a threshold of $3,000 is called *micropurchasing*. The micropurchase threshold for construction subject to the Davis-Bacon Act is $2,000, and the micropurchase threshold for services subject to the Service Contract Act of 1965 is $2,500. When an agency head determines support is needed for contingency operations or to facilitate defense-related operations, the threshold is $15,000 for acquisitions in the United States and $25,000 outside the United States.

Micropurchases may be made from both small and large businesses in the commercial marketplace. But some agencies require that small businesses be used to the maximum extent practicable for micropurchases. Purchases made using the micropurchase method may be made without competition if the agency contracting officer considers the price reasonable. When using the micropurchase method, federal agencies are strongly encouraged to distribute their purchases equitably among qualified vendors.

Small Business Set-Asides Using Simplified Acquisition Procedures

Every open-market acquisition of supplies or services with an anticipated dollar threshold exceeding $3,000, but less than $150,000, is statutorily reserved exclusively for small business concerns, as required by FAR 19.502-2. Acquisitions to support contingency operations or defense-related operations, as determined by the agency head, have a threshold of $250,000 for acquisitions in the United States and $1 million outside the United States. To set aside such an acquisition, the contracting officer must have a reasonable expectation that the agency will receive offers from two or more small business concerns that are competitive in terms of price, quality, and delivery. If there is no expectation of receiving two or more offers, the acquisition may not be set aside for small business concerns.

Subcontracting Plan Requirements

Large companies have the financial resources and expertise to perform contract work for complex, large-dollar acquisitions, but some small businesses also are capable of providing the required services as subcontractors. The Small Business Act mandates that certain business types be given the maximum practicable opportunity to participate as subcontractors for federal contracts: small businesses, service disabled veteran-owned small businesses, HUBZone small businesses, small disadvantaged businesses, and woman-owned small businesses.

Section 8(d) of the Small Business Act requires subcontracting plans for all negotiated and sealed bidding acquisitions for supplies, equipment, and services costing more than $650,000 and for construction acquisitions costing more than $1,500,000. Each large business that participates in full and open competition for contracts expected to exceed these thresholds must have a subcontracting plan approved by the contracting officer before the contract is awarded. During contract performance, if the contractor fails to comply with the approved subcontracting plan, the contractor is assessed liquidated damages as required by FAR 19.705-7. The liquidated damages the contractor must pay to the government are equal to the cost of each subcontracting goal the contractor failed to achieve.

Subcontracting plans submitted by large companies must include goals for subcontract awards to be made to small business concerns. They must submit one of the following three types of subcontracting plans:

- An individual subcontracting plan that contains separate dollar and percentage subcontracting goals for the entire performance period of a specific contract.

- A master subcontracting plan that has been approved and contains all the required elements of an individual plan except for subcontracting goals. When a master plan is submitted, the contracting officer is required to negotiate the goals to form a total plan, at which time it becomes an individual plan and is valid for the entire performance period of a specific contract.

- A commercial subcontracting plan that covers the vendor's fiscal year and includes goals that have been approved companywide. This type of plan does not require the inclusion of individual subcontracting goals. It must be submitted by vendors that sell commercial supplies or services to the general public for nongovernmental purposes.

As stated in FAR 19.702(b), subcontracting plans are not required:

(1) From small business concerns;
(2) For personal services contracts;
(3) For contracts or modifications that will be performed entirely outside of the United States and its outlying areas; or
(4) For modifications to contracts within the general scope of the contract that do not contain the clause at 52.219-8, Utilization of Small Business Concerns (or equivalent prior clauses; e.g., contracts awarded before the enactment of P.L. 95-507).

RESPONSIBILITIES OF AN AGENCY SMALL BUSINESS OFFICE

The responsibilities of an agency small business office vary from agency to agency, but they are all responsible for ensuring that small business concerns are employed in accordance with agency regulations.

Establishing the Small Business Office

The Small Business Act requires every federal agency authorized to negotiate and award contracts to establish an Office of Small and Disadvantaged Business Utilization. (The Department of Defense now calls this office the Office of Small Business Programs per the National Defense Authorization Act of 2006, P.L. 109-163, Section 904.) One of the agency's assistant secretaries is normally designated as the director of this office and is responsible for establishing the agency's small business program, referred to here as the Small Business Program Office. Most agencies call this program the Office of Small Business Development.

The Small Business Program Office is responsible for ensuring that the agency fulfills its responsibility to provide acquisition opportunities to small businesses. Each Small Business Program Office works closely with SBA to implement the necessary acquisition programs and to ensure that these programs are effective within the agency.

The Government's Goals for Awarding Contracts to Small Businesses

Once a year, each executive federal agency estimates the percentage of contracts it expects to award to small businesses and the associated cost of those contracts. SBA negotiates these estimates with each agency to ensure that small businesses have the maximum opportunity to secure contracts from the federal government. Then, the agency's Small Business Program Office must report the agency's achievements to SBA at the end of each fiscal year. SBA compiles, analyzes, and compares each agency's estimates against the actual results and reports the results to the president of the United States. SBA is responsible for ensuring that the cumulative small business goals for all agencies meet or exceed the governmentwide goals established by statute. The governmentwide goals for awarding contracts to small businesses are as follows:

- 23 percent of prime contracts for small businesses

- 5 percent of prime contracts and subcontracts for small disadvantaged businesses

- 5 percent of prime contracts and subcontracts for woman-owned small businesses

- 3 percent of prime contracts for HUBZone businesses

- 3 percent of prime contracts and subcontracts for service-disabled veteran-owned small businesses.

Unfortunately, these statutory goals are infrequently achieved. The 5 percent goals for small disadvantaged businesses and woman-owned small businesses and 3 percent goals for HUBZone businesses and service-disabled veteran-owned small businesses all count toward the 23 percent goal for all small businesses.

The Responsibilities of Small Business Specialists

The Small Business Program Office within most agencies usually has one or two small business specialists to assist with the functions and duties of the small business program. The specialists are federal government employees and are normally independent of the agency's acquisition program. They are well informed about small business rules and regulations and usually possess a working knowledge of acquisition rules and regulations as well. They know more than anyone else in any agency about small business entrepreneurs, small business policies and procedures, and the small business goals established by SBA. They are the agency's primary point of contact for the small business program and are responsible for coordinating all program matters with the small business communities, SBA, and government acquisition organizations.

For a small business program to be successful, it is extremely important for a small business specialist to coordinate, at a minimum, the following acquisition functions with the responsible acquisition parties:

◆ Identify and recommend small business sources to the contracting officer for particular acquisitions.

◆ Review all acquisition actions that will cost between $3,000 and $150,000 if they will not be reserved for small businesses as mandated by FAR 19.502-2.

◆ Review all acquisition actions over the simplified acquisition threshold of $150,000, and make recommendations to the responsible agency contracting officer regarding set-asides for small businesses.

◆ Review all solicitations costing more than $500,000 for supplies and services and costing more than $1,000,000 for construction to see if subcontracting possibilities exist. If they exist, make recommendations to the responsible agency contracting officer.

◆ Review all proposed prime contractors' subcontracting plans and make the necessary recommendations to the responsible contracting officer.

A small business specialist's other primary responsibilities include but are not limited to the following activities:

◆ Developing and maintaining a program for identifying small businesses

◆ Coordinating with the agency's competition advocate to ensure that the objectives of the small business program are integrated into the agency's overall acquisition program

◆ Participating in the agency's annual advanced acquisition plan to determine acquisition strategies, including small business set-aside and subcontracting possibilities

◆ Coordinating with the agency program and acquisition offices, small business offices in other government agencies, and SBA

◆ Coordinating with the business community.

PART II
The Solicitation Phase

CHAPTER 9

Solicitation and Contract Formats, Provisions, and Clauses

(FAR parts 12, 15, and 52)

Sometimes, federal agencies do not include all the provisions and clauses required by law and regulation in solicitations issued to the public. This may be because the requirement is urgent or the acquisition team isn't aware that certain elements must be included. Regardless of the circumstances, solicitation and contract documents must include the proper provisions and clauses and be prepared in the format required by the FAR to be in compliance with law and regulation.

SOLICITATION FORMATS

The federal government uses two different types of contract formats for most solicitations and contracts. One format, the uniform contract format (UCF), is for the acquisition of supplies and services under the negotiated method of contracting; the other is for the acquisition of commercial items. The contract formats simplify the preparation of solicitations and contracts for the federal agencies.

The Uniform Contract Format

The government uses the UCF for most solicitations and resulting contracts when purchasing supplies and services that cannot be defined as commercial items. Per FAR 15.204, the government is *not* required to use the UCF for the following acquisition actions:

(a) Construction and architect-engineer contracts (see Part 36).
(b) Subsistence contracts.
(c) Supplies or services contracts requiring special contract formats prescribed elsewhere in this regulation that are inconsistent with the uniform format.
(d) Letter requests for proposals (see 15.203(e)).
(e) Contracts exempted by the agency head or designee.

All solicitations for competitive and noncompetitive negotiated contracts must use the UCF pursuant to FAR 15.204-1. The UCF is divided into four parts and has 13 sections labeled by letter, from A to M. Section A of part I is the cover for the solicitation or contract. The provisions in section B through H of parts I, II, and III become part of the contract. Only section K in part IV becomes part of the contract, and it must be incorporated by reference. Sections L, solicitation instructions, and M, on evaluation factors, are not included in the resulting contract. A contract clause may be included in a solicitation when necessary, but a solicitation provision may not be included in a contract. An outline of the UCF appears in Exhibit 9-1.

EXHIBIT 9-1: The Uniform Contract Format (FAR 15.204-1)	
SECTION	**TITLE**
Part I: The Schedule	
A	Solicitation/Contract Form
B	Supplies or Services and Prices/Costs
C	Description/Specifications/Statement of Work
D	Packaging and Marking

	EXHIBIT 9-1: The Uniform Contract Format (FAR 15.204-1) (cont.)	
E	Inspection and Acceptance	
F	Deliveries or Performance	
G	Contract Administration Data	
H	Special Contract Requirements	
Part II: Contract Clauses		
I	Contract Clauses	
Part III: List of Documents, Exhibits, and Other Attachments		
J	List of Attachments	
Part IV: Representations and Instructions		
K	Representations, Certifications, and Other Statements of Offerors or Respondents	
L	Instructions, Conditions, and Notices to Offerors or Respondents	
M	Evaluation Factors for Award	

Part I: The Schedule (Sections A through H)

Section A is the cover sheet for the solicitation of contract. Either Standard Form (SF) 33, *Solicitation, Offer and Award,* or Optional Form 308, *Solicitation and Offer—Negotiated Acquisition,* may be used. SF-33, used for both sealed bids and negotiated contracts exceeding $150,000, is issued with the solicitation and is also used to award the contract. Form 308 is used with the solicitation only when using the negotiated method of contracting.

Section B provides a brief description of the supplies or services to be purchased and states the quantities needed. In addition to the description of the supplies or services, agency contracting officers often place blanks next to the line items; the proposing vendors are asked to fill in the blanks with their prices or costs. Alternatively, contracting officers can request price or cost information in the solicitation. The vendors then must set up their own price or cost format or schedule. Section B also identifies any option rights, such as additional quantities or additional performance periods, that the government intends to exercise at a later date.

Exhibit 9-2 shows a sample section B for an architect–engineer acquisition that requires vendors to fill in the blanks with their own prices. The supplies or services to be purchased are normally identified by contract line item numbers, often called CLINs. The sample section B in Exhibit 9-2 does not require any options because it is a one-time effort.

EXHIBIT 9-2: Sample Section B of the Uniform Contract Format

B-1. Services
The contractor shall perform all work necessary to produce a complete set of construction plans and technical specifications sufficient for the construction of the upgrades in the facilities described in this contract. See section C for the specific description of the work required for this contract.

B-2. Type of contract
This is a firm fixed-price contract for the amount of _____.

B-3. Deliverable items and prices
The contractor shall deliver the following items in accordance with section C (Statement of Work) and section F (Deliveries or Performance) of this contract.

Item #	Quantity/unit	Description	Price
CLIN 1	LT 25%	Construction documents	$_____
CLIN 2	LT 50%	Construction documents	$_____
CLIN 3	LT 100%	Final construction	
Total	Document submittals		$_____
CLIN 4	LT monthly progress reports (not separately priced)		

TOTAL firm fixed-price $_____
(Note: CLIN means contract line item number; LT means percent design completion)

B-4. Definition
In this contract, the terms contractor, architect, architect-engineer, and (A/E) are used interchangeably, unless the context indicates otherwise. Each shall mean the contractor identified in block 3A of Standard Form 252, *Architect-Engineer Contract*.

Even though the entire solicitation document is very important, section B is considered critical. Therefore, proposing vendors should be instructed to contact the agency contracting officer in writing if the information is vague or has errors.

Section C describes the government's requirements. It provides detailed, comprehensive descriptions of the supplies or services identified in section B. For example, a brief description in section B may state that the contractor is to produce a complete set of construction plans and technical specifications for the construction of upgrades in a building, as described in section C.

Section C normally contains the statement of work for acquisitions over the threshold of $150,000. Like section B, it is a critical section of the contract, so the language must be clear, concise, and plain—in other words, geared to the general reading public. The proposing vendors should always be asked to notify the contracting officer in writing for clarification if any ambiguities or errors are found. The government must provide its response to all proposing vendors.

Section D describes how the items to be delivered to the government are to be packed, packaged, preserved, and marked. Agency policy or regulation sometimes dictates agency provisions that must be followed for some of the supplies or services being purchased. For some noncomplex acquisitions, this section may be brief. For example, it might read: "Packaging and marking shall be in accordance with commercial practice, except to the extent other requirements are indicated by the security specifications of this contract."

Section E describes the measures the contractor must take to ensure that the delivered supplies or services meet the government's quality requirements. Certain contracts may include provisions that require specialized inspections to be performed only by the government. The quality requirements are sometimes summarized in section C and section I of the contract (which contains contract clauses). That is acceptable, as long as the more specific and detailed provisions appear in section E. The government often uses the standard inspection clauses provided in FAR 46.3 to minimize the cost of inspections. The standard inspection clauses are usually incorporated by reference in the contract because they are long. For more complex acquisitions, some agencies include their own special inspection and acceptance clauses in addition to the clauses required by the FAR.

Section F provides information on the delivery schedule, which lists the items and quantities to be delivered and delivery dates. The period of performance, including any option years, is also specified in this section. Almost all contracts include the following FAR clauses by reference:

◆ 52.242-15, Stop-work order (August 1989)

◆ 52.242-17, Government delay of work (April 1984)

Section G provides information on contract administration. It usually identifies by title the government employee who will be responsible for administering the contract. This section includes information on the preparation and submission of invoices to the government. If required by agency policy and regulation, it also includes the appropriate accounting and appropriation data.

Section H may contain any special contract requirements that are not identified in section I, as permitted by FAR 15.204-2(h). Many agencies include in this section any special agency provisions on government-furnished property or access to government buildings or other provisions that are not covered in section I or other sections of the contract.

Part II: Contract Clauses (Section I)

Section I contains standard clauses required by law and agency provisions when required by agency regulation or policy. The standard clauses are contained in FAR 52.301 (Solicitation Provisions and Contract Clauses (Matrix)), which provides guidance on the use of provisions and clauses. Exhibit 9-3 shows a partial matrix of solicitation provisions and contract clauses. As required by FAR 52.102, the clauses should be incorporated by reference, rather than in full text, to the maximum extent practical. Most agencies include the required clauses by reference and any special provisions required by agency policy or regulation in full text.

EXHIBIT 9-3: Partial Matrix of Solicitation Provisions and Contract Clauses (FAR 52.301)

Key					
P or C	=	Provision or clause	DDR	=	Dismantling, demolition, or removal of improvements
IBR	=	Is incorporation by reference authorized? (see FAR 52.102)	A&E	=	Architect-engineering
UCF	=	Uniform contract format section, when applicable	FAC	=	Facilities
FP SUP	=	Fixed-price supply	IND DEL	=	Indefinite delivery
CR SUP	=	Cost-reimbursement supply	TRN	=	Transportation
FP R&D	=	Fixed-price research and development	SAP	=	Simplified acquisition procedures (excluding micropurchase)
CR R&D	=	Cost-reimbursement research and development	UTL SVC	=	Utility services
FP SVC	=	Fixed-price service	CI	=	Commercial items
CR SVC	=	Cost-reimbursement service			
FP CON	=	Fixed-price construction	Contract Purpose		
CR CON	=	Cost reimbursement construction	R	=	Required
T&M LH	=	Time and material/labor hours	A	=	Required when applicable
LMV	=	Leasing of motor vehicles	O	=	Optional
COM SVC	=	Communication services			

(continues)

EXHIBIT 9-3: Partial Matrix of Solicitation Provisions and Contract Clauses (FAR 52.301) (cont.)

Provision or clause	Prescribed in	P OR C	IBR	UCF	Principal Type or Purpose of Contract																		
					FP SUP	CR SUP	FP R&D	CR R&D	FP SVC	CR SVC	FP CON	CR CON	T&M LH	LMV	COM SVC	DDR	A&E	FAC	IND DEL	TRN	SAP	UTL SVC	CI
52.202-1 Definitions	2.201	C	Yes	I	R	R	A	R	R	R		R	R	R	R		R	R	R	R		R	
52.203-2 Certificate of Independent Price Determination	3.103-1	P	No	K	A		A		A		A			A	A	A	A	A	A	A		A	
52.203-3 Gratuities	3.202	C	Yes	I	A	A	A	A	A	A	A	A	A	A	A	A	A	A	A	A		A	
52.203-5 Covenant Against Contingent Fees	3.404	C	Yes	I	R	R	R	R	R	R	R	R	R	R	R	R	R	R	R	R		R	
52.203-6 Restrictions on Subcontractor Sales to the Government	3.503-2	C	Yes	I	R	R	R	R	R	R									R			R	
Alternate I	3.503-2	C	Yes																				R

Part III: List of Documents, Exhibits, and Attachments (Section J)

Section J contains all the applicable attachments and exhibits for the contract. Per FAR 15.204-4, the title, date, and number of pages for all documents, exhibits, and attachments must be included. When the documents are long and can be found online, it is unnecessary to attach them to the contract. Instead, list the websites from which the documents can be retrieved. Federal agencies can save on publication, printing, or copying costs if the documents can be retrieved from the Internet, and proposing vendors can find the required documents quickly without incurring additional costs. See Exhibit 9-4 for a sample section J.

EXHIBIT 9-4: Sample Section J of the Uniform Contract Format: List of References and Attachments

Title of document	Reference or attachment
P.L. 104-106, Clinger-Cohen Act of 1996 (formerly called Information Technology Management Reform Act)	http://www.tricare.mil/jmis/download/Public Law104_106ClingerCohenActof1996.pdf
P.L. 100-235, Computer Security Act of 1987	http://www.nist.gov/cfo/legislation/Public%20Law%20100-235.pdf
P.L. 106-580, Federal Property Administrative Services Act of 1949, as amended	http://epw.senate.gov/fpasa49.pdf
Agency form for progress report	Attachment 1 in section J
Agency form for contract inspections	Attachment 2 in section J

Part IV: Representations and Instructions (Sections K through M)

Section K contains solicitation provisions that require representations, certifications, and other information that must be submitted by vendors. The required solicitation provisions are included by reference only. The representations and certifications are provided in full text because they have to be completed by the proposing vendors. Proposing vendors must fill in information related to the following FAR clauses, among others:

◆ 52.204-3, Taxpayer identification (October 1998)

◆ 52.204-8, Annual representations and certifications (January 2009)

◆ 52.209-5, Certification regarding responsibility matters (December 2008)

◆ 52.215-6, Place of performance (October 1997).

Upon contract award, section K must be incorporated by reference in the contract.

Section L contains only solicitation provisions that give guidance on the preparation and submission of proposals and on responding to requests for information. Like section C, this is another critical section that must be written in clear, concise, and plain English that the general reading public can comprehend. Proposal preparation instructions that are clear and well organized are the key to obtaining quality proposals. To ensure that the proposing vendors understand the instructions, long sentences and unnecessary verbiage should be avoided.

This section should also identify the type of contracting method to be used and whether the government will be using the trade-off process, the lowest price technically acceptable process, or a combination of both. A combination of the two processes may be used by the National Aeronautics and Space Administration for some of its negotiated acquisitions. For example, the agency could evaluate technical proposals received on a pass/fail basis, and its final selection decision could be based on a trade-off between the vendor's past performance and a cost/price evaluation.

Instructions in section L may ask vendors to organize their proposals in a specific manner—for example, placing administrative, management, technical, past performance, and cost or pricing data in that order. When the government requests a specific proposal format, it is very important that the instructions in section L be compatible with the technical requirements and evaluation factors provided in sections C and M, respectively. The following is an example of proposal volumes that a government agency may ask proposing vendors to submit:

- ◆ Volume 1: Standard Form 33
- ◆ Volume 2: Price proposal
- ◆ Volume 3: Technical proposal
  - › Technical capability and understanding of the requirements
  - › Management/administration plan
- ◆ Volume 4: Past performance.

Section M contains the technical and price evaluation factors for selection of the winning contractor. All significant factors and subfactors to be used in the evaluation process, and their relative importance, must be identified in section M. As required by FAR 15.304(e), the solicitation must state, at a minimum, whether all evaluation factors other than cost or price, when combined, are:

(1) Significantly more important than cost or price;
(2) Approximately equal to cost or price; or
(3) Significantly less important than cost or price (10 USC 2305(a) (3)(A)(iii) and 41 USC 253a(c)(1)(C)).

Like sections B, C, and L, section M is critical. Once again, the language must be clear and concise so that it can be understood by the public. It must also be compatible with the preparation and submission instructions in section L and the technical requirements in section C.

Format for Commercial Items

The federal government simplified the acquisition process by encouraging agencies to take advantage of supplies and services available in the commercial marketplace. The statutes at 41 USC 264(b) and 10 USC 2377(b) promote the acquisition of commercial items and mandate the head of an agency to ensure that acquisition officials acquire them to the maximum extent practicable. FAR part 12 prescribes the policies and procedures that must be used for the acquisition of commercial items and, when appropriate, in conjunction with the policies and procedures in Part 13, Simplified Acquisition Procedures; Part 14, Sealed Bidding; and Part 15, Contracting by Negotiation.

The contract format for commercial items was simplified by Section 8002 of Public Law 103-355 (41 USC 264 note), as implemented in FAR 12.301(a), which requires that contracts for commercial items, to the maximum extent practicable, include only clauses that are:

> (1) Required to implement provisions of law or executive orders applicable to the acquisition of commercial items; or
> (2) Determined to be consistent with customary commercial practice.

The required format for commercial acquisitions appears in FAR 12.303 (Contract Format). This format must be used for acquisitions that are expected to exceed the simplified acquisition threshold of $150,000. Although it is not mandatory to use the commercial format for commercial acquisitions below the simplified acquisition threshold, federal agencies are permitted to use it and often do. Five main sections compose the commercial contract format:

- ◆ Section A: the cover sheet, Standard Form 1449, *Solicitation/ Contract/Order for Commercial Items*

- ◆ Section B: the continuation of blocks 10, 18B, 19, 20, and 25 of SF-1449 if more information is required

- ◆ Section C: the commercial contract clauses required by FAR 12.301

- ◆ Section D: any required contract documents, exhibits, or attachments

- ◆ Section E: the solicitation provisions required by FAR 12.301.

FAR 12.301 provides provisions and clauses for the acquisition of commercial items. These provisions and clauses, often called *acquisition boilerplate*, are developed from laws and regulations and must be included in commercial solicitations and contracts, either in full text or only by reference. The only solicitation provisions and contract clauses that may be used for commercial items are:

- **FAR 52.212-1 (Instructions to Offerors).** This boilerplate provision may be tailored and is incorporated only by reference in section E.

- **FAR 52.212-2 (Evaluation—Commercial Items).** This provision is inserted in section E of the solicitation only when evaluation factors are to be used. Paragraph (a) of the provision must be tailored as required by FAR 12.602.

- **FAR 52.212-3 (Offeror Representations and Certifications—Commercial Items).** This provision may *not* be tailored and is attached to the solicitation in full text in section E.

- **FAR 52.212-4 (Contract Terms and Conditions).** This boilerplate clause may be tailored and must be included by reference only in section C of solicitations and contracts.

- **FAR 52.212-5 (Contract Terms and Conditions Required to Implement Statutes or Executive Orders—Commercial Items).** This clause may *not* be tailored and is included by reference only in section C of solicitations and contracts.

Exhibit 9-5 gives a complete summary outline of the commercial solicitation format.

EXHIBIT 9-5: Solicitation Format for Commercial Items (FAR 12.303)

Section A: Cover sheet
Standard Form 1449—Solicitation/Contract/Order for Commercial Items

Section B: Continuation of SF-1449, if needed
- Block 10 for small business set-aside
- Block 18B for remittance address
- Block 19 for contract line item numbers
- Block 20 for schedule of supplies/services
- Block 25 for accounting data.

Section C: Contract clauses
- FAR 52.212-4, Contract Terms and Conditions—Commercial Items
- Addendum to FAR 52.212-4, if any
  › 52.252-2, Clauses Incorporated by Reference
  › FAR clauses incorporated in full text
- FAR 52.212-5, Contract Terms and Conditions Required to Implement Statutes and Executive Orders—Commercial Items.

Section D: Contract documents, exhibits, or attachments
Attachment A: description and specifications/work statement

Section E: Solicitation provisions
- FAR 52.212-1, Instructions to Offerors—Commercial Items (incorporated by reference)
- Addendum to FAR 52.212-1, Solicitation Provisions (if any)
  › 52.252-1, Solicitation Provisions Incorporated by Reference
  › 52.252-2, Clauses Incorporated by Reference (if to be included in the contract
- FAR 52.212-2, Evaluation—Commercial Items, or other description of evaluation factors for award when appropriate (incorporated by reference)
- FAR 52.212-3, Offeror Representations and Certifications—Commercial Items (incorporated in full text).

WHERE TO FIND PROVISIONS AND CLAUSES

FAR parts 1 through 51 provide policies and procedures for various parts of the federal acquisition process. The provisions and clauses in FAR part 52 (Solicitation and Contract Clauses) were developed to supplement these policies and procedures. FAR part 52 provides the text (boilerplate) for solicitation provisions and contract clauses. The policies and procedures in FAR parts 1 through 51 dictate the provisions or clauses from FAR part 52 that must be included in solicitations and contracts when using the UCF. For example, FAR 16.105

(Solicitation Provisions) requires the contracting officer to insert FAR 52.216-1 (Type of Contract) into a solicitation, unless the acquisition is for information or planning purposes or for a fixed-price simplified acquisition. This provision will be inserted into section L (Instructions, Conditions, and Notices to Offerors or Respondents) in part IV. Upon award, the provision must be deleted from the contract.

The matrix in FAR 52.301 lists provisions and clauses for inclusion in solicitations and contracts for supplies and services that identify the contract purpose as required ("R"); required when applicable ("A"); optional ("O"); and revision ("√"). These text provisions and clauses are based on laws and regulations and are included in solicitations and contracts either in full text or by reference only. The provisions should be included only in solicitations. The clauses are to be included in contracts, but they may be included in solicitations when they will be made part of the resulting contract.

CHAPTER 10

Source Selection and Technical Evaluation Plans

(FAR 15.3)

When reviewing bid protests, the Government Accountability Office (GAO) often finds that the evaluation procedures specified in solicitations are not used in the evaluation of proposals. An agency acquisition covered by the Trade Agreements Act was recently protested by Tiger Truck, LLC. The protest was sustained by the comptroller general in January 2009 (B-400685, January 14, 2009). The agency had failed to follow the required evaluation procedures, which included requirements of the Trade Agreements Act. Sometimes an agency evaluation team will not follow the evaluation procedures or will not use all the evaluation criteria because they were poorly drafted or too general in content. The evaluation criteria must be prepared with great care so that they fit the requirements in the statement of work (SOW). The care with which the criteria are prepared will contribute to the quality of the evaluation and the supplies or services received.

THE PURPOSE OF THE EVALUATION PLAN

The purpose of a source selection plan or technical evaluation plan is to define the approach for evaluating proposals solicited from vendors. The plan serves as a guide for the evaluation team. It denotes team members' roles and responsibilities and establishes the standards of conduct to be maintained by the team, from preparation of the requirements through the award of the contract. The evaluation plan is used for both technical and nontechnical proposals received from vendors in competitive and noncompetitive negotiated acquisitions.

PREPARING THE SOURCE SELECTION AND TECHNICAL EVALUATION PLANS

The government must prepare an evaluation plan that describes how it will assess the quality of each proposal and determine the technical capability of the proposing vendors.

Evaluation Criteria in the Solicitation

A formal evaluation plan for the selection of a vendor is essential for all evaluation processes for acquisitions over the simplified acquisition threshold. Formal evaluation procedures described in FAR part 15 may be used but are not mandatory. Each plan must reflect the complexity of the acquisition. For complex acquisitions, this plan is formally structured and is commonly referred to as a *source selection plan*. For less complex acquisitions, the term *technical evaluation plan* is commonly used. Both the source selection plan and technical evaluation plan should be developed before the solicitation is prepared. Alternatively, the technical evaluation plan can be prepared at the same time as the solicitation for less complex acquisitions.

The criteria in a source selection or technical evaluation plan provide a uniform basis for grading or scoring the proposals. They also keep the evaluators within a defined set of standards, preventing them from making subjective judgments. (The FAR and other procurement statutes use the term *evaluation factors and subfactors*, but many federal agencies use the term *evaluation criteria* and *criterion*. *Criteria* and *criterion* are used in this book.)

The evaluation criteria included in the source selection or technical evaluation plan must be included in the solicitation before publicizing the acquisition. The entire evaluation plan should never be included in the solicitation. Only the evaluation criteria and the description of their relative importance as identified in the evaluation plan may be released. Much of the information in the evaluation plan is considered proprietary, and thus it cannot be released to competing vendors.

The evaluation plan contains, among other information, the criteria to be used for the evaluation of proposals received from vendors. The evaluation criteria included in the solicitation explain to proposing vendors how they will be evaluated. All proposals must be evaluated in accordance with the evaluation criteria described in the solicitation that was released to the public.

There are many variations in the format and content of source selection or technical evaluation plans within the federal sector. See Exhibit 10-1 for a sample formal source selection plan for large, complex acquisitions.

EXHIBIT 10-1: Sample Source Selection Plan

I. Acquisition Background and Objectives
a. Statement of need: *Provide the purpose of the proposed contract.*
b. Applicable contractor conditions: *Describe the capabilities the contractor must possess.*
c. Period of performance: *Identify the length of the contract including all options.*
d. Cost: *Describe cost/price estimate and attach the estimate document.*
e. Method of determining best value: *State whether the trade-off method or lowest price technically acceptable method is to be used.*

II. Plan of Action
a. Competition: *Provide information on who will be competing for the contract.*
b. Evaluation and source selection procedure: *Describe the evaluation criteria, such as technical capability, the vendor's management/administration plan, and past performance.*
c. Contracting consideration: *Describe the contracting method and associated actions.*
d. Budgeting and funding: *Provide information on funding for the contract.*
e. Management information requirement: *Describe internal management responsibilities for the contract.*
f. Logistics consideration: *Provide information on personnel and equipment for the contract and the responsible party for each element.*
g. Milestone schedule: *Provide contract schedule.*
h. Participants in acquisition process: *List names of contracting officer, negotiator, program office representative, and head of the contracting activity or designee.*

Exhibit 10-2 is an example of a very simple, downsized technical evaluation plan for smaller, less complex acquisitions. This sample should be used in a lowest price technically acceptable source selection process, in which proposals are evaluated against the criteria specified in the solicitation and deemed technically acceptable or unacceptable. These samples are just two of many models used by the federal acquisition community.

EXHIBIT 10-2: Sample Technical Evaluation Plan Using the Lowest Price Technically Acceptable Source Selection Process

Introduction
Provide information on the purpose of the plan, the supplies or services to be provided under the resulting contract, the source selection process to be used, and how the proposals will be evaluated.

Rating method
Provide information on the rating or scoring method to be used.

Instructions
Provide specific instructions on rating each criterion and what should be included in the written narrative that supports each rating.

Technical Evaluation Rating Sheets
Request for proposal (RFP) number: _____
Vendor: _____
Evaluator:_____
Overall rating:_____

Instructions
Explain how rating/scoring sheets are to be completed.

Criterion 1: Prior experience and past performance
___ **Acceptable:** All technical requirements of the criterion are met.
___ **Unacceptable**: The vendor's proposal does not fulfill the requirements or include enough information to determine whether the requirements have been met.
Narrative statement supporting rating:_____

Criterion 2: Qualifications of proposed staff
___ **Acceptable:** All technical requirements of the criterion are met.
___ **Unacceptable**: The vendor's proposal does not fulfill the requirements or include enough information to determine whether the requirements have been met.
Narrative statement supporting rating:_____

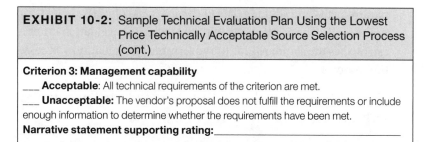

EXHIBIT 10-2: Sample Technical Evaluation Plan Using the Lowest Price Technically Acceptable Source Selection Process (cont.)

Criterion 3: Management capability
___ **Acceptable**: All technical requirements of the criterion are met.
___ **Unacceptable:** The vendor's proposal does not fulfill the requirements or include enough information to determine whether the requirements have been met.
Narrative statement supporting rating:_____

The Party Responsible for the Evaluation Plan

The source selection or technical evaluation plan is prepared by the designated requirements team in the program office that is requesting the acquisition. If needed, the contracting officer will help the team develop the plan. The requirements team should prepare the technical or source selection plan and submit it to the contracting officer before the solicitation is issued. Ideally, it should be submitted with the acquisition request from the program office so that there is no delay in issuing the solicitation. When warranted by urgent and compelling circumstances, the technical evaluation plan can be prepared after issuance of the solicitation as long as the evaluation criteria and their importance are specified in the solicitation. If the technical evaluation plan is prepared after the solicitation is issued, it must be submitted to the contracting officer before vendors' proposals are received.

Developing Evaluation Criteria and Using the SOW

After the SOW, the most important component of the federal acquisition process, the evaluation criteria used to evaluate vendor proposals are the second most important. These criteria should be developed in the very early stages of the acquisition process.

When developing the criteria, the requirements team must review the SOW thoroughly. Because the SOW is the foundation of a solicitation and a standard for measuring the contractor's performance, it must be used as a baseline for structuring reasonable and effectual technical evaluation criteria. The criteria should comply with the requirements and should relate to the goals and objectives identified in the SOW. The SOW, along with the technical evaluation criteria, establishes the standards for the government's evaluation and selection process.

The government's evaluation criteria must be in line with FAR 15.304(b):

> (b) Evaluation factors and significant subfactors must—
> (1) Represent the key areas of importance and emphasis to be considered in the source selection decision; and
> (2) Support meaningful comparison and discrimination between and among competing proposals.

(Most federal agencies use the term *criteria* instead of *factors*.)

The evaluation criteria will help the evaluation team determine which proposal represents the best value and will be most advantageous to the government. This decision results in the award of the contract, so the criteria must be developed with great care.

The criteria chosen will directly affect the quality of the supplies or services received. They must be specific, detailed, and identified in sequential order of importance in the solicitation so that they are clear and meaningful to the proposing vendors and to the government evaluation team. Proposing vendors must be able to understand the bases on which their proposals will be evaluated. Listing the criteria in order of relative importance will help vendors understand the government's priorities.

Broad Discretion in the Selection of Evaluation Criteria

Government agencies have broad discretion in the selection of the evaluation criteria and their relative importance. The number and types of criteria used depend on the government's requirements and on the method that will be used to select the proposal with the best value.

The evaluation criteria should be brief but detailed enough so that the relative importance of each criterion is apparent. Criteria should be limited to the most important requirements so that the government evaluators can perform the evaluation without diluting the grading or scoring of the proposals. Including too many evaluation criteria can complicate or prolong the evaluation process, which can lead to scoring inaccuracies. For example, evaluators faced with a long list of inessential criteria might inadvertently give a vendor an undeserved high score. The contracting officer would probably select that vendor, even though its proposal did not present the best value to the government. In short, it is important to keep evaluation criteria to a manageable number.

Cost or Price and Non-Cost Factors

Although selecting evaluation criteria and determining their relative importance are within the government's discretion, FAR 15.304(c)(1) states that price or cost must be evaluated in every source selection. Therefore, price or cost must be included in the government's evaluation criteria.

FAR 15.304(c)(2) requires the use of non-cost factors. One or more of the following non-cost evaluation criteria must be considered in all source selections to help determine the quality of the supplies or services being acquired:

- ◆ Past performance
- ◆ Compliance with solicitation requirements
- ◆ Technical excellence
- ◆ Management capability
- ◆ Personnel qualifications
- ◆ Prior experience.

Past performance must be evaluated for all negotiated competitive acquisitions over the simplified acquisition threshold of $150,000, unless the contracting officer determines that such an evaluation is not appropriate for the acquisition. If past performance is deemed to be an inappropriate criterion, the contracting officer is required to document the reasons it is not appropriate and was not included in the evaluation process. When past performance is included as an evaluation criterion, some agencies evaluate it on a pass/fail basis and exclude it from the rating method used for the acquisition. The approach used for evaluating past performance must be described in section M of the solicitation.

RANKING OF CRITERIA

The evaluation criteria chosen must be put in order of relative importance before they are made part of the evaluation plan and the solicitation. Two levels of relative importance must be specified in the solicitation. The first level, as required by 41 USC 253a(c)(1)(C) and 10 USC 2305(a)(3)(A)(iii) and as implemented in FAR 15.304(e), is the relationship between cost or price and non-cost criteria. The statute states that the vendors must be told whether the combined non-cost or price criteria are:

> (i) significantly more important than cost or price;
> (ii) approximately equal in importance to cost or price; or
> (iii) significantly less important than cost or price.

Per statute (41 USC 253a (b)(1)(A) and (B)), the solicitation must also include a statement that specifies the relative importance of each non-cost or -price criterion. This is the second level of relative importance. The non-cost criteria should always be listed in descending order of importance.

For most acquisitions, technical capability is the most important criterion. The following text on the relative order of importance is an example of what might appear in section M of a solicitation:

M-3. Evaluation Criteria: Relative Order of Importance
The following five criteria will be evaluated in order of importance. All non-price factors are listed in descending order of importance, with the most important criterion listed first. Criteria 1–5

combined are significantly more important than price. Price will not be scored, but its reasonableness and realism will be evaluated.

1. Technical approach/management plan
2. Past performance
3. Corporate experience
4. Key personnel
5. Quality assurance.

If the government expects to select the lowest-priced technically acceptable proposal, the solicitation must clearly state that award will be made on that basis: The winning proposal will be the one that meets the government's minimum standards at the lowest cost or price. When non-cost criteria are more important than cost, the solicitation must inform vendors that cost is secondary to quality and that the government will compare the combined non-cost criteria and will accept a proposal based on factors other than lowest price.

Proposal Rating Methods

FAR 15.305(a) permits the federal government to use "…any rating method or combination of methods that include color or adjectival ratings, numerical weights, and ordinal rankings." The two primary rating methods used by the government to evaluate proposals are numerical scoring and adjectival rating. Each agency, civilian and military, has internal policies regarding the use of the two methods, and some do not encourage the use of the numerical scoring method.

The rating method chosen establishes a defined set of measures for evaluators to use when rating proposals and provides a valid foundation for ranking proposals. Proposal evaluation may be performed by one individual or by a team from the program office that requested the acquisition. The size of the evaluation team depends on the size and complexity of the acquisition.

Numerical Scoring Method

When using the numerical scoring method, each criterion and any subcriteria are assigned a point value. The combined total for cost or price and non-cost criteria usually add up to 100 points. (Some agencies do not score costs.) A rating card is often used to score proposals.

When the criteria are not of equal importance, they should be listed in the order of importance, preferably in descending order of importance. When all the criteria are of equal importance, the solicitation should state this. The point value for each criterion should be included. If a cost or price criterion is *not* assigned numerical points, the solicitation should inform vendors whether the combined non-cost evaluation criteria (technical criteria) are more important than cost or price, of equal importance to cost or price, or less important than cost or price.

Exhibit 10-3 suggests sample language that may be included in a solicitation when the numerical scoring method is used. This language is only an example. It is not considered appropriate for or applicable to all acquisition actions.

EXHIBIT 10-3: Sample Solicitation Language
(Numerical Scoring Method)

The government will award a contract to the responsible vendor whose offer will be most advantageous to the government, price and other evaluation criteria considered. The following criteria, in descending order of relative importance, will be used to evaluate proposals submitted to the government.

Technical criteria	60 points
Cost/price criteria	40 points
Past performance	Rated as satisfactory or unsatisfactory

1. Technical criteria
Describe how each subcriterion below will be evaluated.
A. Technical approach
B. Personnel (employee) experience
C. Understanding of the requirements

2. Cost/price evaluation criteria: Describe how cost or price will be evaluated.

3. Past performance: Describe how past performance will be evaluated.

Adjectival Rating Method

The adjectival rating method is sometimes referred to as *adjectival description of importance*. Based on how well the vendor's proposal has met the evaluation standards, each of the stated criteria is rated using four or five descriptors such as "excellent," "good," "fair," and "poor," or "exceptional," "acceptable," "marginal," or "unacceptable." Normally, each criterion is given an adjectival rating; these are then summarized into one rating for the proposal.

Exhibit 10-4 provides sample language that may be included in a solicitation when the adjectival rating method is used. This language is only an example. It is not considered appropriate for or applicable to all acquisition actions.

EXHIBIT 10-4: Sample Solicitation Language
(Adjectival Rating Method)

The government will award a contract to the responsible vendor whose offer will be most advantageous to the government, price and other criteria considered. Adjectival ratings—"exceptional," "acceptable," "marginal," or "unacceptable"—will be used to indicate the degree to which the proposals meet the evaluation criteria. The following criteria, in descending order of relative importance, will be used to evaluate proposals.

1. Cost/price criteria
Describe how the cost/price proposal will be evaluated.

2. Technical criteria
Describe how each subcriterion below will be evaluated.
A. Technical approach
B. Personnel (employee) experience
C. Understanding of the requirements

3. Past performance
Describe how past performance will be evaluated. State that past performance will be rated as satisfactory or unsatisfactory.

Technical Evaluation

A technical evaluator or evaluation panel will review, study, and investigate the proposal based on the technical evaluation criteria the government identified in the solicitation and on the complete technical evaluation plan that was not released to the vendors. The criteria will help determine the suitability of the supplies or services to be provided. It will also help the evaluators select the vendor whose proposal represents the best value for the federal government.

The evaluation criteria set forth in the solicitation are the only criteria that may be used in evaluating the vendor proposals. Using other criteria will only lead to vendor protests, which will be sustained by the Government Accountability Office and the U.S. courts. The contracting officer is responsible for ensuring that the evaluation is carried out in accordance with the criteria identified in the solicitation and technical evaluation plan.

FAR 15.305(a) gives specific instructions on the evaluation of proposals:

> Proposal evaluation is an assessment of the proposal and the offeror's ability to perform the prospective contract successfully. An agency shall evaluate competitive proposals and then assess their relative qualities solely on the factors and subfactors specified in the solicitation. Evaluations may be conducted using any rating method or combination of methods, including color or adjectival ratings, numerical weights, and ordinal rankings. The relative strengths, deficiencies, significant weaknesses, and risks supporting proposal evaluation shall be documented in the contract file.

Cost/Price Evaluation

As required by FAR 15.304(c)(1), cost or price is always part of the government's evaluation process. All cost or price to the government as received from proposing vendors requires some form of cost or price evaluation.

The cost or price evaluation is the contracting officer's responsibility. When needed and upon request, the Defense Contract Audit Agency (DCAA) will assist the contracting officer with this evaluation. This agency is responsible for performing the necessary audit analysis of proposing vendors' financial and accounting records.

In performing a cost or price evaluation, the contracting officer must consider the reasonableness, realism, and completeness of the prices proposed. Cost realism analysis is usually performed to ensure that the proposed prices are compatible with the requirements identified in the solicitation and the proposed technical approach. When a price proposal contains unreasonable, unrealistic, or unbalanced costs or prices, it is the responsibility of the contracting officer to take the necessary corrective action. For example, the contracting officer may deem the proposal to be unacceptable and remove the proposing vendor from further competition, or he or she may simply downgrade the proposal.

When vendors are asked to submit costs for option periods specified in the solicitation, the costs for both the base year and option periods must be evaluated.

CHAPTER 11

Legal Review during the Solicitation Phase

(FAR 1.602-3, 4.8; 14.407-3, 14.407-4, 15.303, 42.12, part 33, 37.103, 37.104, part 49)

A recent audit performed by an agency inspector general revealed that an acquisition office had made a conscious decision not to comply with agency policy requiring legal review of solicitations because its solicitations were not being reviewed on time. Other acquisition audits also have reported that solicitations are not being reviewed for legal sufficiency prior to issuance. Some acquisition organizations skip the legal review process for solicitations because they are not aware of its benefits.

A legal review ensures that a solicitation and related transactions are in compliance with acquisition laws and are legally defensible in case of a protest. Every acquisition professional is responsible for reviewing agency regulations and policies on legal sufficiency reviews and complying with them. This chapter discusses the legal review process for solicitations, which should be followed by all acquisition professionals. A legal review (also called a *legal sufficiency review*) is not a technical review. Rather, it is a review that determines whether a solicitation and related transactions are lawful. Legal departments commonly assume that the technical information in a solicitation is in compliance with agency regulation and policy, so no review of the technical content is performed unless requested by the contracting officer.

LEGAL OFFICES AND REVIEWS

Each of the 15 large federal agencies formally called executive departments has legal departments or offices that employ a dedicated team of legal professionals.

Legal Counsel or Team

Each agency's designated legal office for acquisitions is responsible for providing necessary legal reviews and advice about acquisition matters to the acquisition community. Legal offices usually help the acquisition community with the preparation, negotiation, and interpretation of contracts, grants, cooperative agreements, and other associated matters. They sometimes offer advice and recommendations to agency program officials and other technical personnel during the administration phase of awarded contracts. In addition, they are often tasked with reviewing and commenting on agency acquisition rules and regulations, policies and procedures, and executive orders from the president of the United States.

The agency-designated legal counsel or team is responsible for reviewing solicitations and associated transactions to ensure that all documentation to be released to the public is in compliance with acquisition laws, rules, and regulations and with executive orders from the president of the United States. When performing reviews for legal sufficiency, legal counsel focuses on compliance with statutory and regulatory requirements as well as good contracting practices. Counsel often makes an extra effort to ensure that acquisition transactions are clearly written and provide detailed descriptions of the supplies or services to be purchased.

Legal Sufficiency Review Requests

Agency contracting officers are in the best position to seek legal advice for agency solicitations. They are responsible for deciding which solicitations need legal review and submitting a request for review to the responsible legal office. Advice and legal review should be requested for solicitations to ensure that they are legally sufficient when:

- There is liability or risk in the transaction.
- The transaction is complex and highly technical.
- The transaction is of a very high dollar value.
- The transaction is of utmost importance to the mission of the agency.

The request for legal sufficiency review should be made in writing.

Dollar Threshold for Legal Review

Many agencies require legal review for solicitations, basic ordering agreements, and interagency agreements when the dollar threshold exceeds the simplified acquisition threshold of $100,000. And some agencies require legal sufficiency review for highly technical, complex solicitations that are below the $150,000 threshold. For example, a contracting officer may request a legal sufficiency review for an information technology solicitation with a threshold as low as $10,000 if the acquisition is deemed technically complex.

For some small organizations, such as bureaus within large federal agencies, legal sufficiency reviews are required for the purchase of noncommercial supplies or services costing at least $300,000. The general threshold for a legal sufficiency review for the purchase of commercial supplies or services is usually $2 million.

WHERE TO FIND INSTRUCTIONS ON LEGAL REVIEW

All 15 federal agencies (executive departments) have acquisition regulations that provide guidance on acquisitions and related transactions, as authorized by FAR 1.301. Acquisition regulations developed by agencies may implement or supplement the FAR and may include agency policies, procedures, contract clauses, solicitation provisions, and forms. Agency policies and procedures are limited to those necessary to implement the FAR. They are indexed to the FAR so that they coincide with FAR policies and procedures.

Executive Departments' Acquisition Regulations

The FAR does not provide instructions on legal sufficiency reviews for solicitations and related transactions, but many agencies have their own instructions for the legal review of solicitations. These instructions are provided in the agency's regulation or are issued by its acquisition policy office.

The 15 agencies listed in Exhibit 11-1 all have agency acquisition regulations. However, some of these agency regulations do not have instructions on the procedures for legal sufficiency reviews. Acquisition regulations and other information for each agency can be found online at http://www.usa.gov/Agencies/Federal/Executive .shtml#vgn-executive-departments-vgn.

Acquisition regulations are often called *department acquisition regulations*. For example, the acquisition regulation for the Department of State, called the Department of State Acquisition Regulation (DOSAR), can be found on the State Department's website at http://www.statebuy.state.gov/dosar. Instructions for legal reviews for the Department of State can be found in subpart 604.71 (Procurement Quality Assurance Program) of DOSAR.

EXHIBIT 11-1: Executive Departments (Federal Agencies)	
Department of Agriculture (USDA)	Department of Commerce (DOC)
Department of Defense (DoD)	Department of Education (ED)
Department of Energy (DOE)	Department of Health and Human Services (HHS)
Department of Homeland Security (DHS)	Department of Housing and Urban Development (HUD)
Department of the Interior (DOI)	Department of Justice (DOJ)
Department of Labor (DOL)	Department of State (DOS)
Department of Transportation (DOT)	Department of Treasury
Department of Veterans Affairs (VA)	

Agency Policies

In addition to the agency acquisition regulations that implement and supplement the FAR, each agency has acquisition policies and procedures that have been developed specifically for its federal acquisition community. These internal acquisition policies and procedures usually provide detailed instructions on the legal review process for solicitations and related transactions, even if the agency's acquisition regulation does not provide guidance.

Office of the Procurement Executive

Agency acquisition regulations, including internal acquisition policies and procedures, can always be obtained from the agency's Office of the Procurement Executive. The regulations and policies are under the direct control of the agency *procurement executive*, who is responsible for managing the acquisition system for the agency. The procurement executive has the authority to prescribe and promulgate policies, regulations, and standards for the federal acquisition community. The procurement executive, in concert with the office of legal counsel and the head of the contracting activity, is responsible for developing and monitoring acquisition processes, including legal sufficiency reviews, to ensure that all acquisition actions are of high quality and are performed in a timely and cost-effective manner.

PART III

The Evaluation, Negotiation, and Award Phase

CHAPTER 12

Technical and Cost or Price Evaluations

(FAR 1.102-2(c), 3.104-3, 9.505-3, 12.5, 14.201-6, 15.3, and 15.6)

The third phase of the federal acquisition process is known as the evaluation, negotiation, and award phase. In recent years, vendors protested several large acquisitions because evaluations were not performed based on the agency's evaluation procedures, and the protests were sustained by the Government Accountability Office (GAO). A technical evaluation of a vendor's proposal must be performed against the evaluation criteria specified in the solicitation and the government's requirements. When the evaluation is not performed in accordance with the evaluation criteria and the requirements provided in the solicitation, competing vendors will certainly protest it.

THE PURPOSE OF EVALUATIONS

An evaluation is done to assess the quality of a proposing vendor's offer and to determine whether the vendor is capable of performing the work at a reasonable price for the government. The evaluation process begins when proposals are received from proposing vendors, and it continues through the negotiation process and the evaluation of the revised final proposals.

The number of evaluators participating depends on the size and complexity of the acquisition. Just one technical evaluator may work on a small acquisition; an evaluation team or panel may be assembled if the acquisition is large and complex.

THE IMPORTANCE OF INTEGRITY AND FAIRNESS

All government acquisition professionals are required to exercise sound business judgment when purchasing supplies and services from vendors in the commercial marketplace. They are also required to conduct business with integrity, fairness, and openness. The guiding principles for conducting business with private-sector vendors are specified in FAR 1.102-2(c)(3):

> The Government shall exercise discretion, use sound business judgment, and comply with applicable laws and regulations in dealing with contractors and prospective contractors. All contractors and prospective contractors shall be treated fairly and impartially but need not be treated the same.

It is essential that the federal government as an entity maintain public trust. It is even more important that the actions of each proposal evaluator reflect integrity and fairness during the source selection phase. Proposing vendors are entitled to fair and impartial treatment in the source selection process, and they have a right to unbiased award decisions.

Every once in a while, an unsuccessful vendor protests a contract award, alleging that the government's source selection procedure was biased. These vendors, however, rarely win their cases because protests of this nature are hard to prove.

THE TECHNICAL EVALUATION PROCESS

Proposals received from competing vendors must be evaluated based on the evaluation criteria and the requirements set forth in the solicitation issued to the public. The evaluation also must follow the procedure outlined in the evaluation plan during the solicitation stage of the acquisition process. The contracting officer, who appoints the technical evaluator or evaluation team, is responsible for ensuring that the evaluation is carried out in accordance with the criteria identified in the solicitation and the technical evaluation plan.

Briefing the Evaluation Team

The contracting officer is responsible for briefing the technical evaluator or evaluation panel on the procedures for conducting the evaluation. The briefing takes place after proposals are received from competing vendors. It must cover, at a minimum, the following:

- ◆ Overview of the solicitation document
- ◆ Handling of the technical evaluation plan
- ◆ Standards of conduct and requirements governing conflicts of interest
- ◆ Government security requirements
- ◆ Deadline for submitting evaluation reports
- ◆ Handling of classified and protected material.

Once the contracting officer briefs the technical evaluation team on its responsibilities, each team member is asked to sign a conflict of interest and nondisclosure agreement. This agreement must comply with section 27 of the Office of Federal Procurement Policy Act (Procurement Integrity Act), 41 USC 423, as implemented in FAR 3.104. The act forbids individuals responsible for evaluating proposals in anticipation of making an award to:

- ◆ Disclose any vendor proposal information or source selection information before award is made
- ◆ Have any financial interest in proposing vendors' companies or their affiliates
- ◆ Have made future employment arrangements with proposing vendors and their affiliated companies.

Quick Review of Initial Proposals

When vendor proposals arrive, the evaluation team and the contracting officer perform an initial screening of the documents. This initial screening is not a thorough review of the proposals. During this period, the evaluators:

◆ Make sure that the proposals are organized correctly and are properly identified

◆ Ensure that the price data is separated from the technical information, preferably in a separate volume

◆ Confirm that proposals are complete and in compliance with the instructions provided in the solicitation

◆ Determine whether particular vendors must be asked to provide information that is missing from the proposals.

Evaluation teams sometimes perform a quick complete review of the proposals to immediately eliminate from further consideration those that are deemed to be extremely deficient. This method is not recommended for large, complex requirements because they require the evaluation of many criteria.

After the initial screening, the evaluation team performs a thorough detailed evaluation and establishes a competitive range. Once the competitive range is established, proposals that are severely deficient are eliminated.

Evaluating Proposals Based on the Evaluation Plan and Criteria

Federal agencies may evaluate proposals in any manner, as long as evaluations are performed with fairness and impartiality and in accordance with the evaluation plan, particularly the evaluation criteria identified in the solicitation. If, for example, the solicitation stated that the award will be made to other than the lowest-priced offeror or other than the offeror with the highest technical rating, the evaluation team must use the trade-off process. When the trade-off process is used, FAR 15.305(3) requires that the following elements be included in the evaluation record:

> (i) An assessment of each offeror's ability to accomplish the technical requirements; and
>
> (ii) A summary, matrix, or quantitative ranking, along with appropriate supporting narrative, of each technical proposal using the evaluation factors.

The evaluation team will use the lowest price technically acceptable source selection process if the solicitation informed vendors that award would be made to the vendor whose proposal was technically acceptable and had the lowest evaluated price. To be technically acceptable, the proposal must meet the minimum requirements specified in the solicitation. The vendor with the lowest price among those meeting the minimum requirements is awarded the contract.

Each proposal must be evaluated independently by each member of the evaluation team when the acquisition is not complex and has a small dollar threshold. (Alternatively, it may be evaluated by a single person.) The evaluators must assess the relative quality of each vendor's solutions and how well it fulfills the criteria and subcriteria identified in the solicitation. During the evaluation process, members of the evaluation team may not compare notes or discuss the proposals with one another. All questions and concerns should be directed to the technical evaluation chairman or designee, as identified in the evaluation plan, and the responsible contracting officer.

The Competitive Range

When each proposal has been evaluated and rated against the evaluation criteria, the team gives the results to the contracting officer. If discussions are to be held, the contracting officer must establish a competitive range that includes the highest-rated proposals before holding the discussions.

Determining the competitive range is a two-step process. The first step is to identify the top-rated proposals. If the acquisition team—the evaluation team and the contracting officer—determines that the number of proposals in the competitive range is too large for efficient competition, the contracting officer may limit the number of vendors in the range. An acquisition team may limit the number of vendors in the competitive range only if the solicitation includes a provision informing competing vendors that the competitive range may be limited for the sake of efficiency. If vendors are not notified of this option, the government must include all highly rated proposals in the competitive range.

The competitive range must be established based solely on the criteria specified in the solicitation, per FAR 15.306(c). Nonetheless, cost or price may be used as determining factors when necessary to include or exclude proposals from the competitive range because the FAR does not preclude their use.

Each vendor whose proposal is eliminated from further consideration must be notified in writing right away, preferably the next day, by the responsible contracting officer. Unsuccessful vendors must also be informed that they are eligible for a preaward debriefing if they request it in writing within three days from receipt of the notification. The contracting officer may conduct the preaward debriefing right away or may wait until after contract award, as permitted by regulation.

Discussion of Deficiencies and Weaknesses

After the competitive range is established, discussions, sometimes called negotiations, are held independently with each vendor whose proposal is in the competitive range. The government may award a contract without discussions, but a provision that informs competing vendors that award may be made without discussions must be included in the solicitation.

FAR 15.306(d)(2) explains the purpose of holding discussions: "The primary objective of discussions is to maximize the Government's ability to obtain best value, based on the requirement and the evaluation factors set forth in the solicitation." Discussions are held between competing vendors and the government primarily to allow the vendors to correct any deficiencies and significant weaknesses that the evaluation team documented during the evaluation process. The government often asks vendors to revise their proposals, giving them an opportunity to improve their quality.

Discussions with vendors on the deficiencies and significant weaknesses found in their proposals must be meaningful. It is extremely important to make a distinction between the terms *deficiency* and *significant weakness*. FAR 15.001 defines both terms:

> "Deficiency" is a material failure of a proposal to meet a Government requirement or a combination of significant weaknesses in a proposal that increases the risk of unsuccessful contract performance to an unacceptable level.

> "Weakness" means a flaw in the proposal that increases the risk of unsuccessful contract performance. A "significant weakness" in the proposal is a flaw that appreciably increases the risk of unsuccessful contract performance.

Deficiencies documented during the evaluation process are usually found in proposals that do not meet the government's minimum requirements. Documented weaknesses are usually flaws found in proposals that meet the minimum requirements specified in the solicitation.

Sometimes, discussions cover not only deficiencies and significant weaknesses but also adverse performance information. When a vendor has an unacceptable past performance record, the contracting officer must discuss it with the vendor. This must be mentioned in the solicitation if it is to be a topic of discussion. The government may request clarification or interpretation of ambiguous technical information or additional information when a vendor's proposal lacks sufficient information on the vendor's technical, management, or performance approach. It is not necessary to discuss every part of a proposal that needs improvement. The contracting officer is responsible for determining the extent and scope of these discussions.

Whether discussions are oral or written, they must be held independently with each vendor. Discussions with vendors in the competitive range must be conducted with integrity and fairness. A vendor's technical information and pricing may not be revealed to other vendors in the competitive range without its permission. Any information provided by vendors competing for government contracts may not be released to the public without the vendor's permission.

Submission and Evaluation of Final Proposals

When discussions are completed, each vendor is given an opportunity to submit a revised proposal. A revised proposal was once called a *best and final offer*, but the term was changed to *final proposal revision* in 1997. The contracting officer requests that final proposal revisions be submitted by a specific date and time. Vendors may be given as little as one week or as long as one month to submit their final revised proposals. The time allowed for submission of final proposal revisions depends on the type and complexity of the acquisition.

Once the government receives the final proposals, the evaluation team performs the final evaluation. When the final evaluation is complete, the team usually convenes to discuss its findings and tries to reach a consensus on the technical merits of each proposal.

Acquisition rules and regulations were designed to allow the federal government to obtain the best supplies or services at the best prices. The statutes at 41 USC 253a(c)(1)(B) and 10 USC 2305(a)(3)(ii) require the government to consider cost or price in the evaluation of proposals. Every solicitation issued under the full and open competition method of contracting should include price as an evaluation criterion, per FAR 15.304(c)(1), which implements these two statutes. GAO, in its review of bid protests, has repeatedly held that price must be an evaluation criteria for an acquisition to be in compliance with the statutory competition requirement and that price must be given meaningful consideration. GAO has stated many times that price serves as a reasonable basis for contract award.

The evaluation of cost or price proposals is the responsibility of the contracting officer, but it is sometimes necessary to get advisory assistance from the technical evaluation team. When an agency receives proposals, the technical proposals are given to the evaluation team. The contracting officer retains the cost or price proposals if the technical proposal is a standalone document. When a technical proposal is intimately related to the information in the cost proposal—for example, labor hours are discussed in the technical proposal and the associated costs in the cost proposal—it may be necessary to provide the cost or price proposal to the technical team. In a situation like this, the contracting officer is responsible for determining the appropriate solution.

The contracting officer usually withholds cost or price proposals from the technical team in order to keep team members from being influenced by cost as they evaluate the technical proposals. Once the technical evaluation is complete, the contracting officer gives the cost or price proposals to the technical evaluation team to review the data. This cost or price review of each proposal allows the team to determine:

- ◆ If the cost or price proposed is what the government should realistically pay for the proposed work

- ◆ Whether the proposed cost or price reflects an understanding of the requirements specified in the solicitation

- ◆ Whether the proposed cost or price is consistent with the various elements of the associated technical proposal.

The contracting officer usually compiles a cost or price evaluation report to establish prenegotiation objectives before negotiating with the vendor whose proposal offers the best value to the government. Establishing prenegotiation objectives will help determine a fair and reasonable price for both the government and the vendor awarded the contract.

Protest: The Evaluation Plan Was Not Followed

If an unsuccessful vendor protests a contract award, and it is determined that the agency did not follow its own evaluation plan, the protest will certainly be sustained. For example, on March 11, 2008, the Boeing Company protested the award of a contract to Northrop Grumman Corporation for replacing the aging KC-X aerial refueling tankers for the United States Air Force. The Boeing Company submitted its protest (B-311344, et al., June 18, 2008) to GAO, and upon review, the protest was sustained in June 2008. The comptroller general found that the Air Force had failed to evaluate the aerial refueling tanker proposals in accordance with the requirements and evaluation criteria identified in the solicitation and did not conduct discussions in a fair and equitable manner. Based on the protest findings, the Air Force was asked to:

- Reopen discussions with the proposing vendors

- Obtain revised proposals

- Reevaluate the revised proposals

- Make a new source selection decision.

The findings of the comptroller general appear verbatim in Exhibit 12-1.

Award probably will not be made for this acquisition for two or three years, simply because the proposals were not evaluated in accordance with the evaluation criteria specified in the solicitation. It is obviously essential, then, that technical and price proposals be evaluated in accordance with the agency's evaluation plan, especially with regard to the evaluation criteria specified in the solicitation, as required by regulation. Failure to do this will result in a bid protest, causing unnecessary delays in the delivery of the needed supplies or services.

The acquiring agency reserves the right to decide which vendor will provide the best value to the government, but only as long as it complies with statutory and regulatory requirements that mandate full and open competition and fairness to competing vendors.

EXHIBIT 12-1: Summary of Aerial Refueling Tanker Acquisition Protest Decision (B-311344, et al., June 18, 2008)

The comptroller general found a number of errors in the evaluation of proposals by the U.S. Air Force and discussions it held with the vendors competing for a tanker contract. The comptroller general sustained the protest based on the following seven errors, repeated here verbatim from the comptroller general's decision report:

(1) The Air Force did not evaluate the offerors' technical proposals under the key system requirements subfactor of the mission capability factor in accordance with the weighting established in the RFP's evaluation criteria.

(2) A key technical discriminator relied upon in the selection decision in favor of Northrop Grumman relating to the aerial refueling area of the key system requirements subfactor, was contrary to the RFP.

(3) The Air Force did not reasonably evaluate the capability of Northrop Grumman's proposed aircraft to refuel all current Air Force fixed-wing, tanker-compatible aircraft using current Air Force procedures, as required by the RFP.

(4) The Air Force conducted misleading and unequal discussions with Boeing with respect to whether it had satisfied an RFP objective under the operational utility area of the key system requirements subfactor.

(5) Northrop Grumman's proposal took exception to a material solicitation requirement related to the product support subfactor.

(6) The Air Force did not reasonably evaluate military construction (MILCON) costs associated with the offerors' proposed aircraft consistent with the RFP.

(7) The Air Force unreasonably evaluated Boeing's estimated non-recurring engineering costs associated with its proposed system development and demonstration (SDD).

The comptroller general indicated that, except for the errors found, the Government Accountability Office believed that Boeing would have had a substantial chance of being selected for award. On July 8, 2008, the Pentagon announced that it would reopen the acquisition bidding process on the $35 billion contract for the refueling tankers. On September 10, 2008, the Department of Defense terminated the current competition for the air force airborne tanker replacement because the award could not be made by January 2009. It was determined by the secretary of Defense that the best course of action was to give the new federal government administration full flexibility regarding the acquisition of new tankers.

A copy of the comptroller general's legal decision and recommendations can be found at http://www.gao.gov/decisions/bidpro/311344.htm.

Protest: Cost/Price Was Not Considered

In 1997, a solicitation was issued by the Department of Energy (DOE) to replace five expiring incumbent contracts for advisory and assistance support services. SCIENTECH, Inc., a competing vendor, filed a protest with GAO after it was excluded from the competitive range (B-277805.2, January 20, 1998). The company contested that the agency's evaluation of its proposal was unreasonable and that the proposal was improperly excluded from the competitive range. DOE did not consider vendors' cost or price in determining the competitive range, even though the solicitation stated that contracts were to be awarded based on proposing vendors' performance approach and their fulfillment of the government's cost/rate criteria. The protest was sustained by the comptroller general, who stated the following:

> We sustain the protest because DOE, in making its competitive range determination, unreasonably failed to consider cost or price as well as significant relevant past performance information that was highlighted in SCIENTECH's proposals.

The SCIENTECH decision indicates that it is improper to eliminate a proposing vendor from the competitive range based only on technical considerations and that cost or price must be considered as an evaluation criterion. A proposal may be included in the competitive range if it is considered to be technically acceptable and the cost or price is within range of the independent government cost estimate. But if the cost or price is too high and cannot be reduced, or it is too low, the proposal is usually not included in the competitive range.

The government is not bound to its initial decision to include certain proposals in the competitive range. It may remove any proposal that was originally included in the competitive range. This is supported by FAR 15.306(c)(3), which states:

> If the contracting officer, after complying with paragraph (d)(3) of this section, decides that an offeror's proposal should no longer be included in the competitive range, the proposal shall be eliminated from consideration for award. Written notice of this decision shall be provided to unsuccessful offerors in accordance with 15.503.

The government has broad discretion in determining which proposals may be included or excluded within the competitive range. However, the government may not use a predetermined cutoff score to determine the competitive range. The government's decision is usually not contested unless it is found to be not fair or reasonable.

THE EVALUATION REPORT

There is no statutory or regulatory guidance on the preparation of the required evaluation report. However, one of the basic rules for evaluating proposals appears in FAR 15.305(a): ". . . The relative strengths, deficiencies, significant weaknesses, and risks supporting proposal evaluation shall be documented in the contract file."

The technical evaluation team is responsible for reviewing and evaluating technical proposals. Evaluation of cost or price proposals and past performance information is performed by the contracting officer. Because acquisition rules and regulations do not require any specific methodology to be used for these evaluations, most agencies follow the basic rules for evaluating proposals provided in the FAR, along with their own internal policies and procedures.

Each evaluation team member must document his or her review and analysis of each proposal using the criteria and relative weighting specified in section M of the solicitation. Evaluation plans usually include a technical evaluation form that each member of the team uses to review, analyze, and rate each proposal. Team members note narrative comments on the strengths, weaknesses, deficiencies, and risks of each proposal on the form. The form should be prepared when the evaluation criteria are developed and before the solicitation is issued. Exhibit 12-2 shows a basic, simplified sample technical evaluation form.

EXHIBIT 12-2: Sample Technical Evaluation Form

Instructions

Evaluation will be based on the criteria specified in section M of the solicitation. The criteria below are keyed to section M. You must rate each proposing vendor's fulfillment of the evaluation criteria numerically, provide comments that support the rating, and document the strengths and weaknesses of each proposal.

Criterion 1: Technical capability
(Select one.)
High: *(Insert points and description of what constitutes a high rating.)*
Medium: *(Insert points and description of what constitutes a medium rating.)*
Low: *(Insert points and description of what constitutes a low rating.)*

Narrative comments
(Describe deficiencies and weaknesses as well as strengths of the proposals.)

Criterion 2: Management capability
(Select one.)
High: *(Insert points and description of what constitutes a high rating.)*
Medium: *(Insert points and description of what constitutes a medium rating.)*
Low: *(Insert points and description of what constitutes a low rating.)*

Narrative comments
(Describe deficiencies and weaknesses as well as strengths of the proposals.)

Criterion 3: Staff experience
(Select one.)
High: *(Insert points and description of what constitutes a high rating.)*
Medium: *(Insert points and description of what constitutes a medium rating.)*
Low: *(Insert points and description of what constitutes a low rating.)*

Narrative comments
(Describe deficiencies and weaknesses as well as strengths of the proposals.)

The Summary Report

Upon completion of the evaluation, the technical team meets to discuss, and reach a consensus on, the technical merits of each proposal. During the consensus period, each evaluator is normally allowed to change the scores or written comments he or she made during the evaluation period. See Exhibit 12-3 for a sample consensus form that can be completed by an evaluation team for each proposal. Like the sample technical evaluation form, this is a basic, simplified sample and is only one version of many used by the federal government.

EXHIBIT 12-3: Sample Technical Evaluation Consensus Form

Solicitation number _____

Name of company _____

1. Technical evaluation criteria

A. Criterion 1: Technical capability

Total score: _____

Comments: _____

_____

B. Criterion 2: Management capability

Total score: _____

Comments: _____

_____

C. Criterion 3: Staff experience

Total score: _____

Comments: _____

_____

The consensus report and each evaluation report are turned over to the chairman or leader of the technical team so that he or she can prepare the technical evaluation summary report.

The summary report is based on individual team members' documented evaluation findings and on the consensus report. For small, noncomplex, relatively low-cost acquisitions, only one or two evaluators are needed to perform the evaluation, so there is usually no chairman or team leader to prepare the summary report. Usually, summary reports are not necessary for these types of acquisitions.

The summary report consists of a narrative summary of the evaluation findings and technical rankings of all proposals evaluated. The technical rankings, based on the consensus of the evaluation team, are usually listed in descending order of technical merit. Because the designated source selection authority relies heavily on the summary report when making the source selection, the report must provide current, accurate information. In addition to the evaluation findings and technical rankings, the report also specifies whether each proposal is acceptable or not acceptable for selection.

The report may also recommend awarding the contract to a particular vendor. Most agencies do not discourage evaluation teams from recommending the vendors they believe should receive a contract. Acquisition laws and regulations are silent on whether those performing proposal evaluations may make source selection recommendations.

Once completed, the summary report, along with the individual evaluation reports, is submitted to the contracting officer for review. He or she may request a debriefing on the report and, when necessary, further clarification or explanation. Exhibit 12-4 shows an example of the data usually presented in a technical evaluation summary report. The accompanying narrative should be brief (one or two pages long) but comprehensive.

EXHIBIT 12-4: Technical Evaluation Summary Report					
Vendor	**Technical and management expertise**	**Corporate experience**	**Past performance**	**Overall technical rating**	**Price**
Company 1	Exceptional	Very good	Very good	Very good	$160,099,000
Company 2	Very good	Very good	Very good	Very good	$140,708,738
Company 3	Satisfactory	Marginal	Neutral	Satisfactory	$130,595,900
Company 4	Satisfactory	Satisfactory	Neutral	Satisfactory	$128,600,800

Based on the ratings and prices, Company 4 will be awarded the contract if the solicitation had a provision that informed vendors the award would be made to the vendor with the lowest-priced technically acceptable proposal. But if section M of the solicitation stated that all evaluation factors other than cost or price are significantly more important than cost or price when combined, award would mostly likely be made to Company 1. The solicitation language would have permitted a trade-off among cost or price and non-cost technical criteria, allowing the government to award to a vendor other than the one with the lowest-priced proposal.

Selecting the Source

There are no specific statutory standards governing the source selection decision. The statutes at 41 USC 253b(d)(3) and 10 USC 2305(b)(4)(C) require only that federal agencies make the award promptly to the responsible source whose proposal is most advantageous to the government, considering only cost or price and other factors included in the solicitation. FAR 15.308 (Source selection decision) states that the source selection authority's decision must be based on a comparative assessment of proposals against all criteria in the solicitation. It also provides guidance on documenting the source selection decision:

> . . . The source selection decision shall be documented, and the documentation shall include the rationale for any business judgments and trade-offs made or relied on by the SSA [source selection authority], including benefits associated with additional costs.

> Although the rationale for the selection decision must be documented, that documentation need not quantify the trade-offs that led to the decision.

Once all evaluations are completed, the source selection authority selects a vendor for contract award. The agency contracting officer acts as the source selection authority unless the agency head has appointed another individual, which is sometimes done for very large-dollar, complex acquisitions.

The source selection authority often gives serious consideration to a vendor recommendation made by the technical evaluation team. The selection must be based only on the evaluation reports and the evaluation team's suggestions. The decision must be rational and consistent with the evaluation criteria specified in the solicitation.

The source selection decision document must show that the decision was not arbitrary, that it was based on sound judgment, and that there was a reasonable basis for the selection. If the source selection decision is not adequately documented and a vendor files a protest with the agency or GAO, the protest will most likely be sustained because there is a lack of sufficient information.

Upon making a selection and documenting the decision, the contracting officer makes the award to the vendor whose proposal offered the best value and is most advantageous to the government, price and other factors considered. The award must be made promptly and the vendor notified in writing or by electronic means. Notification of contract award must always made be in writing—never orally. The contract award document must be signed by both parties, and the contractor cannot begin work until it has a legally binding contract.

Vendors in the competitive range that were not awarded the contract must be notified in writing within three days after the award, per FAR 15.503(b)(1). This written notification, called a postaward notice, is issued by the contracting officer. Upon written request, the contracting office must brief vendors that were in the competitive range but did not receive the contract award. The technical and cost evaluation reports, including the summary report and past performance information, are used for the debriefing. Chapter 17 offers a detailed explanation of the notification and debriefing process.

CHAPTER 13

Determining Price Reasonableness

(FAR 8.4, 12.209, 13.106-3, 13.202, 14.408-2, 15.4, and 15.305)

The government requires contractors to be paid fair and reasonable prices. There is no set definition for the term "fair and reasonable," and obtaining a fair and reasonable price depends on many factors. Also, the process of determining price reasonableness is sometimes not adequately documented or supported, so the basis for a determination of price reasonableness may not be apparent. In one audit, the Government Accountability Office (GAO) found that the price reasonableness determinations for 25 out of 49 contract actions were not properly documented or supported. GAO also found that some agencies had added work to existing contracts without determining whether the prices for the new work were fair and reasonable.

A good cost or price analysis and good business judgment help agencies make a good determination of price reasonableness. The purpose of this chapter is to help the acquisition professional understand the processes involved in determining a fair and reasonable price.

THE PURPOSE OF DETERMINING PRICE REASONABLENESS

Federal agencies are required to treat federal contractors fairly and to pay fair and reasonable prices for the supplies or services the contractors provide. The purpose of determining price reasonableness is to ensure that the federal government actually pays fair and reasonable prices. The FAR requires that a cost or price analysis be performed for each acquisition action before the contract is awarded to determine whether the price offered by each proposing vendor is fair and reasonable.

Fair and reasonable is defined in FAR 31.201-3 (Determining Reasonableness):

> A cost is reasonable if, in its nature and amount, it does not exceed that which would be incurred by a prudent person in the conduct of a competitive business . . . the burden of proof shall be upon the contractor to establish that such cost is reasonable.

The term *fair and reasonable* may have different meanings to the federal government, which is mainly interested in saving taxpayer dollars, and vendors, which are interested in making as much money as possible. Even though each party may interpret the term differently, a good price or cost analysis will help the contracting officer and the vendor reach an agreement on a fair and reasonable price for the work.

OBTAINING COST OR PRICING DATA

Before issuing a solicitation, the government must determine whether it requires cost or pricing data. Before requesting this data, the contracting officer is required by regulation to explore every means available to ascertain whether a fair and reasonable price can be determined. Requesting cost or pricing data unnecessarily is not encouraged because it increases proposal preparation costs, requires the vendors and the government to assign additional staff to the acquisition action, and may extend the preaward phase of the acquisition. The data requires certification by the vendor as required by FAR 15.406-2 (Certificate of Current Cost or Pricing Data).

Solicitation Provision for Cost or Pricing Data

Every solicitation issued by the government must provide instructions on the type of data to be submitted by proposing vendors. Section L of the solicitation should specify the type of cost or price information that proposing vendors must submit so that the government can perform the appropriate analysis. FAR 15.403-5(a) requires the contracting officer to first consider the type of information needed. Once the government's needs have been determined, the contracting officer must indicate in the solicitation:

> (1) Whether cost or pricing data is required;
> (2) That, in lieu of submitting cost or pricing data, the offeror may submit a request for exception from the requirement to submit cost or pricing data;
> (3) Any information other than cost or pricing data that is required; and
> (4) Necessary preaward or postaward access to offeror's records.

Requesting Cost or Pricing Data

Regulations generally require that cost and pricing data be submitted to the government for large, negotiated contracts. Cost and pricing data is not required when the government determines in the early stages of an acquisition that there will be adequate price competition. If it is determined that adequate competition will not be available, FAR 15.403-4 requires the submission of cost and pricing data for all acquisition actions that have thresholds of $700,000 and beyond, unless an exception applies. All exceptions to the cost or pricing data requirement must be justified in writing and approved by the head of the contracting activity. As required by FAR 15.403-1(a), cost and pricing data is not required for acquisitions at or below the simplified acquisition threshold of $150,000. Data other than cost and pricing data may be obtained if the government determines that it is necessary for determining price reasonableness or cost realism.

When a proposing vendor is asked to submit cost or pricing data, its price proposal must provide cost breakdowns for basic cost elements and must be certified by the vendor as accurate, complete, and current. This means that the data must be factual and be the basis for pricing judgments made by the proposing vendor. The vendor must submit a signed certificate of current cost or pricing data verifying the accuracy, completeness, and currency of the data.

Formats for Submitting Cost and Pricing Data

When cost or pricing data is required, the contracting officer may ask proposing vendors to use one of three methods to prepare and submit their proposals:

- The format shown in FAR 15.408 (Table 15-2: Instructions for Submitting Cost/Price Proposals When Cost or Pricing Data Are Required)

- An alternative format with proposal preparation instructions specified by the contracting officer

- The vendors' own cost or pricing formats.

Requesting Other Data

A contracting officer may request information other than cost or pricing data in order to determine whether the costs or prices offered by vendors are fair and reasonable. *Information other than cost or pricing data* is information that is necessary to determine price reasonableness or cost realism for cost-reimbursement contracts. This information does not have to be certified as accurate, complete, and current by the proposing vendors. The vendors usually determine the level of detail and how the information is formatted, unless the solicitation describes a specific format that must be used. Most vendors provide a level of cost detail similar to certified cost and pricing data, although this is not required.

The contracting officer is forbidden to request or obtain cost or pricing data in the following situations:

- When the acquisition is at or below the simplified acquisition threshold of $150,000 (unless deemed necessary)

- When prices are based on full and open competition

- When prices are based on prices set by law or regulation

- If prices for option years will be negotiated at award time

- When commercial items are being purchased, unless the offered price cannot be determined to be fair and reasonable

- When the head of the contracting activity waives the requirements (in exceptional cases)

- When modifying contracts or subcontracts for commercial items.

COST ANALYSIS

Federal agencies are required to perform cost analysis when they receive requested cost or pricing data from proposing vendors. A vendor's cost or pricing data represent the estimated expenses it anticipates incurring while performing the work requested by the government. The required cost analysis helps the government determine the reasonableness of the estimated costs.

Acquisitions over the Simplified Acquisition Threshold

The contracting officer may determine that it is essential to perform a cost or price analysis for a negotiated acquisition over the simplified acquisition threshold of $150,000. (Sealed bids, however, never require cost analysis.) This analysis ensures that the government does not pay prices that are unreasonably high or low.

An unreasonably low proposal price could mean that the vendor made a clerical error, did not understand the work, or is buying in. *Buying in* is a term used when a vendor submits an offer that is below the estimated cost of an acquisition. If a vendor with a buy-in proposal receives the contract award, it will probably try to recover its losses by increasing the contract price through unnecessary contract modifications. Sometimes the government inadvertently allows proposals considered to be buy-ins into the competitive range.

Reviewing Separate Cost Elements

It is often difficult to determine whether a vendor's price is fair and reasonable if it is not based on competitive commercial pricing. Therefore, some form of analysis, such as cost analysis, may be necessary for making a price reasonableness determination. *Cost analysis* is used to determine the reasonableness of the estimated cost of the work to be performed—*not* the reasonableness of the contract price. FAR 15.404-1(c)(1) defines cost analysis as follows:

> Cost analysis is the review and evaluation of the separate cost elements and profit in an offeror's or contractor's proposal (including cost or pricing data or information other than cost or pricing data), and the application of judgment to determine how well the proposed costs represent what the cost of the contract should be, assuming reasonable economy and efficiency.

It is advisable to perform a cost analysis when:

◆ Full and open competition is not used

◆ The award will be made on a sole source basis

◆ Not enough reliable cost information is available to determine whether the price is fair and reasonable.

Cost Realism Analysis

A *cost realism analysis* determines the probable cost of performance, and it helps the acquisition team select a vendor for contract award. The purpose of the cost realism analysis is to determine whether each vendor's proposed costs:

◆ Are what the government should realistically pay for the work

◆ Reflect a good understanding of the government's requirements, as stated in the statement of work (SOW)

◆ Are consistent with the significant elements of the vendor's technical proposal.

A cost realism analysis must be performed for all cost-reimbursement contracts and may also be performed for competitive fixed-price incentive contracts. The costs proposed for cost-reimbursement contracts are only estimates developed by vendors, so a cost realism analysis must be performed to determine whether the vendor's proposed costs are realistic. Sometimes, the probable cost, as determined by the cost realism analysis, differs from the vendor's costs. The independent government cost estimate must be used to determine best value when performing a cost realism analysis. The probable cost should reflect the independent government estimate.

Acquisition regulation does not require the government to conduct an in-depth analysis or to verify each and every item when performing a cost realism analysis. However, the government must perform a comprehensive cost realism analysis of all major cost elements in order to reasonably determine that the proposed costs are consistent with the vendor's technical approach and are realistic for the work to be performed.

The methodology used for the cost realism analysis must instill some level of confidence the proposed costs are reasonable and realistic. FAR 15.404-1(c)(2) suggests six techniques and procedures for a cost realism analysis that will help ensure a fair and reasonable price. However, there is no single standard process used for federal acquisitions. Each cost realism analysis is unique and demands careful review and evaluation.

Although the review and evaluation of a price proposal is strictly the responsibility of the acquisition personnel, it is a team effort and may require some input from the technical evaluation team, federal government auditors, and agency pricing analysts.

The Cost Analysis Process

It is helpful to have a standard sequence of steps to follow when performing a cost analysis. This sequence provides some consistency for the specialists doing the analysis, the team members assisting with the analysis, and those who will read the cost evaluation report. The following steps are considered essential when performing a cost analysis.

- ◆ Review each price proposal to ensure that it is complete, based on the proposal submission instructions in the solicitation.

  - ➤ If a proposal is incomplete, immediately obtain the necessary cost information from the vendor.

- ◆ Compare the costs cited in each proposal with the independent government cost estimate, actual costs incurred by the vendor for previous or current contracts, and previous cost estimates from the competing vendors for the same or similar items.

- ◆ Ensure that inefficient or uneconomical practices from the vendor's cost history are not included in the vendor's price proposal.

- ◆ Compare the costs against a recent audit of the vendor, or if necessary, request a new audit on the proposed costs.

- ◆ Ensure that costs submitted are in compliance with FAR part 31 (Contract Cost Principles and Procedures) and, if applicable, the cost accounting standards found in 48 CFR Ch. 99.

Cost Elements Used to Establish Prenegotiation Objectives

A cost analysis is used to develop a negotiation position that will help the contracting officer and the vendor expected to be awarded the contract reach an agreement on a fair and reasonable price. When cost analysis is required, the following cost elements must be reviewed and analyzed to establish the prenegotiation objectives:

- **Direct costs.** Includes labor, scrap, and spoilage material, and other direct costs such as travel, special tooling, consultant services, and other direct charges.

- **Material costs.** Includes materials used in the manufacture of products or used to provide a service, such as raw materials, parts, assemblies, and subassemblies to make a final product. Sometimes it includes scraps allowance. Scrap and spoilage material can be included as a factor of material costs, direct costs, or indirect costs.

- **Overhead or indirect costs.** Includes charges that may not be charged as direct costs, such as selling expenses, general and administrative expenses, and other charges that fall under overhead cost. The terms *overhead* and *indirect costs* are sometimes used interchangeably.

- **General and administrative costs (G&A).** Includes the costs to a company for doing business. It may include taxes, supplies, equipment rental, telephone bills, electricity bills, and other miscellaneous expenses.

- **Profit or fee.** The additional money a contractor receives after all costs have been paid.

- **Total price.** Includes all costs and profit or fee.

Documenting the Cost Analysis

Exhibit 13-1 shows a sample cost analysis. The cost analysis must be documented and filed in the government's contract file. The document can be used for planning future acquisition actions and may be used as reference material if a disgruntled vendor files a protest.

EXHIBIT 13-1: Sample Cost Analysis (FAR 15.404-1(c))

Request for proposal (RFP) number _____

Background of the government's requirement

Brief description of supplies or services

Cost analysis

Perform the analysis and establish both the main and higher negotiation objectives for each cost element. The higher cost objective should not exceed the highest amount the government is willing to accept.

Cost element	Vendor's offer	Government's main objective	Government's higher cost objectives	Reference notes
Direct costs				A
Material costs				B
Overhead/ indirect costs				C
G&A				D
Total costs				E
Profit/fee				F
Total price				G

Direct costs (Reference A)
Review and examine each direct labor cost and other direct costs specifically associated with the work to be performed. The costs proposed by the vendor should be in line with the government's requirements. Provide a brief summary of the analysis.

Material costs (Reference B)
Review and examine the contractor's sources and estimates of direct material costs, such as vendor purchase orders, quotes from vendor competitions, catalog items, prior history, and other appropriate sources. Only material that becomes a part of the finished work or is used to perform the work may be considered direct material. Provide a brief summary of the analysis.

Overhead/indirect costs (Reference C)
The terms overhead *and* indirect costs *are sometimes used interchangeably. Examine the breakdown of the vendor's estimate of its overhead costs to ensure they are allowable and allocable. Review the rates used and determine whether they are reasonable. Discuss the actual rates used in previous contracts and any ceiling rates proposed by the vendor. Provide a brief summary of the analysis, and specify whether the rates used are reasonable.*

EXHIBIT 13-1: Sample Cost Analysis (FAR 15.404-1(c)) (cont.)

G&A (Reference D)

General and administrative (G&A) costs are another indirect cost of doing business. Examine the contractor's pool of G&A expenses to ensure they are allowable and allocable. Review the proposed rates by year to determine whether they are reasonable. Provide a brief summary of the analysis, and specify whether the G&A pool has been determined to be reasonable.

Total costs (Reference E)

Calculate and identify the total costs or total expenses the vendor will incur in performing the contract work.

Profit/fee (Reference F)

Use the government agency's profit/fee structured approach. If there is no structured approach, the six major factors identified in FAR 15.404-4(d) must be considered to arrive at a fair profit/fee rate and amount. The six factors used to determine a reasonable profit are (1) contractor effort, (2) contract cost risk, (3) federal socioeconomic programs, (4) capital investments, (5) cost control and other past accomplishments, and (6) independent development.

Total price (Reference G)

Calculate and identify the total price (costs + profit or fee).

PRICE ANALYSIS

The federal government relies on commercial market forces to obtain the best value when purchasing supplies and services. The competitive nature of the marketplace under true full and open competition normally forces vendors to propose fair and reasonable prices. However, competition alone may not be enough to determine whether the prices proposed are fair and reasonable. For example, market conditions may not be the same for all competing vendors, or there may be a limited number of vendors competing for the contract, thus skewing the prices the vendors offer.

Methods of Price Analysis

Price includes the cost of performing contract work plus the profit earned by the contractor. A *price analysis* is a set of methods used to determine whether a proposed price is reasonable. FAR 15.404-1(b)

(1) defines price analysis as "the process of examining and evaluating a proposed price without evaluating its separate cost elements and proposed profit."

The federal government is required to perform price analysis for all acquisitions for which it does not obtain cost or pricing data. When there is adequate competition, a price analysis, not a cost analysis, is performed to determine whether the proposed price is reasonable. Price analysis must be performed when the contract is a firm fixed-price contract or a fixed-price with economic adjustment contract. Price analysis *cannot* be performed for cost-reimbursement contracts because the real price of the contract is known only after the work is completed.

Price analysis is faster than cost analysis; not a lot of data is needed to determine whether a price proposed by a vendor is fair and reasonable. A sound price analysis should be based on several different types of data obtained from as many sources as possible. Prices proposed by competing vendors are considered to be the most important data and are almost always used in performing price analysis. The government frequently uses pricing information from previous price proposals or contracts for the same or similar supplies or services.

There is no single standard process for performing price analysis. FAR 15.404-1(b)(2) suggests seven techniques and procedures that can be used to ensure a fair and reasonable price. The first two are cited as preferred techniques in FAR 15.404-1(b)(3):

> (i) Comparison of proposed prices received in response to the solicitation. Normally, adequate price competition establishes price reasonableness (see 15.403-1 (c) (1)).
> (ii) Comparison of previously proposed prices and previous Government and commercial contract prices with current proposed prices for the same or similar items, if both the validity of the comparison and the reasonableness of the previous price(s) can be established.

When comparing previously proposed prices and previous contract prices with current proposed prices, the following two variables must be taken into consideration:

♦ Current economic conditions and the economic conditions when pricing information was made available

♦ Current quantities needed and quantities purchased under previous contracts.

When competitors' proposed prices are deemed insufficient grounds for determining the reasonableness of a price, or previous contract prices are not available, the remaining five techniques provided in FAR 15.404-1(b)(2) may be used to determine whether a price is fair and reasonable.

♦ **Using parametric data.** Using parametric estimating methods (such as cost per pound) can highlight pricing inconsistencies that warrant additional inquiry.

♦ **Comparing a vendor's price with published prices of supplies or services** sold to the public. This pricing information is available in catalogs and other printed materials.

♦ **Comparing a vendor's price with the government's own independent cost estimate.**

♦ **Comparing a vendor's price with pricing information obtained through market research** for the same or similar items.

♦ **Analyzing price** based on the pricing information provided by the proposing vendor.

The FAR states that the government is not limited to using these seven price analysis techniques. Unfortunately, no further guidance is provided on what other techniques can be used by federal agencies to determine whether prices offered by vendors are fair and reasonable.

Documenting the Price Analysis

The price analysis must be documented and filed in the contract file. It is used to develop objectives for negotiations with the vendor that is expected to be awarded the contract. The document can also be used for planning future acquisition actions and may be used as reference material if an unsuccessful vendor files a protest. Exhibit 13-2, a sample price analysis, shows what this document should contain at a minimum. This format, which can easily be modified, is recommended only for noncomplex, small-dollar acquisitions.

EXHIBIT 13-2: Sample Price Analysis (FAR 15.404-1(b))

Request for proposal (RFP) number _____

Background of the government's requirement

Brief description of supplies or services

Have the supplies or services been previously purchased?
If the supplies or services have been previously purchased, and price reasonableness for the prior contract was established, check the box that is applicable to this acquisition.
_____ Adequate price competition
_____ Catalog or market price
_____ Price analysis
_____ Other *(briefly describe other data or information used to establish price reasonableness)*

ANALYSIS
Price analysis was performed in accordance with FAR 15.404-1(b).

Indicate which price analysis techniques were used to establish the proposed price as fair and reasonable.
_____ **Number of price proposals**
Identify the number of proposals received in response to the solicitation. Provide information on whether the price analysis and the use of full and open competition were sufficient to determine that the prices proposed were fair and reasonable.
_____ **Comparison with other contracts**
Describe how the proposed prices compare with other contracts for the same or similar items.
_____ **Use of parametric data**
Discuss whether the use of parametric data (such as cost per pound) revealed significant inconsistencies that warranted further investigation.

EXHIBIT 13-2: Sample Price Analysis (FAR 15.404-1(b)) (cont.)

_____ **Comparison with competitive published price lists or market prices**
Describe the results of the comparison.
_____ **Comparison of proposed prices with the independent government cost estimate**
Describe the results of the comparison.
_____ **Comparison of proposed prices with prices obtained through market research for the same or similar items**
Describe the results of the comparison.

PRICE OBJECTIVES FOR NEGOTIATIONS
Describe the primary price objective that was established based on the analysis.
Also, provide low and high price objectives that can be used during negotiations if needed.

The proposed price has been determined to be fair and reasonable for award based on the price analysis performed.

_____   _____
Contracting officer (signature)   Date

PRENEGOTIATION OBJECTIVES

To reach a price settlement that is fair and reasonable to both the government and the vendor that has been selected to receive the contract, it is absolutely essential to establish prenegotiation objectives before engaging in negotiations. The prenegotiation objectives should be based on the results of the analysis performed on the chosen vendor's technical and price proposals. The scope and depth of the cost or price analysis that supports the negotiation objectives—as well as the negotiations themselves—depend on the importance and complexity of the acquisition.

The contracting officer is responsible for preparing prenegotiation objectives, then conducting negotiations with the chosen vendor. FAR 15.406-1(b) provides the following guidance on establishing the prenegotiation objectives:

> The contracting officer shall establish prenegotiation objectives before the negotiation of any pricing action. The scope and depth

of the analysis supporting the objectives should be directly related to the dollar value, importance, and complexity of the pricing action. When cost analysis is required, the contracting officer shall document the pertinent issues to be negotiated, the cost objectives, and a profit or fee objective.

For the sake of efficiency and organization, the prenegotiation objectives should be included in the cost or price analysis documents, as shown in Exhibits 13-1 and 13-2. If there is a preference for a standalone prenegotiation document and if time permits, a separate document may be prepared.

THE PRICE NEGOTIATION MEMORANDUM

When the cost or price analysis is complete, and negotiations with the selected vendor have been held, a price negotiation memorandum must be prepared in accordance with FAR 15.406-3 (Documenting the Negotiation). The price negotiation memorandum is usually prepared by a contract specialist who was a member of the government's requirements team. The FAR guidance states:

a) The contracting officer shall document in the contract file the principal elements of the negotiated agreement. The documentation (e.g., price negotiation memorandum (PNM)) shall include the following:
(1) The purpose of the negotiation.
(2) A description of the acquisition, including appropriate identifying numbers (e.g., RFP No.).
(3) The name, position, and organization of each person representing the contractor and the Government in the negotiation.
(4) The current status of any contractor systems (e.g., purchasing, estimating, accounting, and compensation) to the extent they affected and were considered in the negotiation.
(5) If cost or pricing data were not required in the case of any price negotiation exceeding the cost or pricing data threshold, the exception used and the basis for it.

(6) If cost or pricing data were required, the extent to which the contracting officer—

(i) Relied on the cost or pricing data submitted and used them in negotiating the price;

(ii) Recognized as inaccurate, incomplete, or noncurrent any cost or pricing data submitted; the action taken by the contracting officer and the contractor as a result; and the effect of the defective data on the price negotiated; or

(iii) Determined that an exception applied after the data were submitted and, therefore, considered not to be cost or pricing data.

(7) A summary of the contractor's proposal, any field pricing assistance recommendations, including the reasons for any pertinent variances from them, the Government's negotiation objective, and the negotiated position. Where the determination of price reasonableness is based on cost analysis, the summary shall address each major cost element. When determination of price reasonableness is based on price analysis, the summary shall include the source and type of data used to support the determination.

(8) The most significant facts or considerations controlling the establishment of the prenegotiation objectives and the negotiated agreement including an explanation of any significant differences between the two positions.

(9) To the extent such direction has a significant effect on the action, a discussion and quantification of the impact of direction given by Congress, other agencies, and higher-level officials (i.e., officials who would not normally exercise authority during the award and review process for the instant contract action).

(10) The basis for the profit or fee prenegotiation objective and the profit or fee negotiated.

(11) Documentation of fair and reasonable pricing.

As the person responsible for conducting negotiations, the contracting officer makes the final decision on the contract price that will be negotiated with the chosen vendor and signs the resulting contract. Members of the acquisition team, such as price analysts, engineers, lawyers, and sometimes financial auditors, may participate in the negotiation session and provide assistance in their areas of expertise at the contracting officer's request.

Exhibit 13-3 shows a sample price negotiation memorandum that includes all the elements required by the FAR. It also includes a few additional elements, such as modification type, agency requirement descriptions, delivery dates, and set-aside information, that are considered essential for negotiated acquisition actions. It is not necessary for the contracting officer and the chosen vendor to agree on every element of cost, so some of the cost elements may be reduced and some may be increased during negotiations. The final negotiated cost elements are not usually the same as the prenegotiation cost objectives established during the cost or price analysis period.

EXHIBIT 13-3: Sample Price Negotiation Memorandum (FAR 15.406-3)

1. Purpose of negotiation

This memorandum is to document the negotiations conducted by _____ *(identify office)* for the purchase of _____ *(identify services or supplies)*.

2. Information on the proposed contract

A. Solicitation number

B. Type of action (check one)

_____ Definitive contract

_____ Letter contract

_____ Modification to contract number _____

_____ Change order

_____ Other

C. Description of the requirement

D. Delivery date or performance period

E. Type of competition *(check one)*

_____ Full and open

_____ Other than full and open

_____ Justification for other than full and open competition approved on _____

_____ After exclusion of sources, exception number: _____

_____ Synopsis to government point of entry (GPE) on _____

_____ No synopsis, in accordance with FAR 5.202 (a)

EXHIBIT 13-3: Sample Price Negotiation Memorandum (FAR 15.406-3) (cont.)

F. Set-aside information (FAR 19.5; *check one*)
_____ 100% small business set-aside
_____ Partial set-aside
_____ 8(a)
_____ Unrestricted
_____ Other _____

G. Type of contract (FAR part 16; *check one*)
_____ FFP (16.202)
_____ FP with EPA (16.203)
_____ FPI (16.204)
_____ Cost, no fee (16.302)
_____ CPIF (16.304)
_____ CPAF (16.305)
_____ CPFF (16.306
_____ Indefinite-delivery (16.5)
_____ Time-and-materials (16.601)
_____ Labor-hour (16.602)
_____ Letter contract (16.603)
_____ Other such as incentive contracts (16.4) _____

3. Negotiation conference and participants
Negotiation was conducted between _____ and _____ on *(date)* _____ at
_____ *(location).*

A. Contractor personnel
List name(s), position(s), and organization for each individual.

B. Government personnel
List name(s), position(s), and organization for each individual.

4. Contractor systems
Describe the current status of any contractor systems (e.g., purchasing, accounting) that affected negotiations.

5. Cost or pricing data not required
Certified cost or pricing data was not required, per FAR 15.403-1(b), for the following reasons *(check all that apply):*
_____ Prices are based on full and open competition
_____ Prices were set by law or regulation
_____ Commercial items are being purchased
_____ A waiver was granted by the head of the contracting activity
_____ This is a modification to a contract or subcontract for commercial items

---

EXHIBIT 13-3: Sample Price Negotiation Memorandum (FAR 15.406-3) (cont.)

6. Cost or pricing data required for negotiations at or exceeding $700,000

Certified cost or pricing data was required per FAR 15.403-4. The contracting officer relied on the data submitted and used it in negotiating the price as follows:

_____ Complete reliance

_____ Action was taken on inaccurate, incomplete, or outdated cost or pricing data received

Describe the effects of this data on price negotiation and the action that was taken on the data:

_____ It was determined that an exception applied after the data was received, so the data was no longer considered usable cost or pricing data

7. Results of negotiation

A. Summary of contractor's proposal

B. Field pricing assistance recommendations

C. Price reasonableness based on price analysis

Briefly summarize the source and type of data used. If rate verification was requested, identify the costs that were questioned.

D. Price reasonableness based on cost analysis

Provide a summary of negotiations for each cost element.

Cost element	Vendor's offer	Government's main objective	Government's high objectives	Reference notes
Direct costs				A
Material costs				B
Overhead/indirect costs				C
G&A				D
Total costs				E
Profit/fee				F
Total price				G

Direct costs (reference A)

Material costs (reference B)

Overhead/indirect costs (reference C)

EXHIBIT 13-3: Sample Price Negotiation Memorandum (FAR 15.406-3) (cont.)

G&A (reference D)

Total costs (reference E)

Profit/fee (reference F)

Total price (reference G)

8. Facts/considerations
Describe significant facts or considerations used to establish negotiation objectives and to reach agreement, and explain any differences between the objectives and final agreement.

9. Influences on negotiations
Describe any direction given by Congress, other agencies, and senior executive-level officials and how this affected negotiations.

10. Profit or fee
Describe the basis of the profit or fee established for negotiations and the final profit or fee that was negotiated.

11. Price reasonableness determination
The proposed contract price has been determined to be fair and reasonable based on *(check one)*:
_____ Receipt of adequate price competition, in accordance with FAR 15.403-1(c)(1)
_____ Receipt of certified cost or pricing data in accordance with FAR 15.404-1(c), on which a cost analysis was performed for individual cost elements and a price analysis was conducted, to ensure that the overall price is fair and reasonable.
_____ Price analysis involving the procedures described in FAR 15.404-1(b)
_____ Cost analysis, in accordance with the procedures described in FAR 15.404-1(c)

12. Determination of contractor's responsibility
In accordance with FAR 9.104-1, I hereby determine that _____ *(name of company)* is responsible and has the following qualifications:
(a) The requisite financial resources or ability to obtain them
(b) The ability to comply with the delivery or performance schedule as demonstrated by the vendor
(c) A satisfactory record of performance
(d) A satisfactory record of integrity and business ethics
(e) The necessary organizational experience, accounting and operational controls, and technical skills, or the ability to obtain them
(f) The necessary equipment and facilities
(g) Has been determined to be qualified and eligible to receive the award

EXHIBIT 13-3: Sample Price Negotiation Memorandum (FAR 15.406-3) (cont.)

DETERMINATION

Based on the foregoing, I have determined that award of contract number _____, made with _____ *(contractor's name)* in the amount of $_____, for the period of _____, is in the best interest of the government, and the price is fair and reasonable.

_____

Contracting officer's name

_____

Signature

_____

Date

CHAPTER 14

Determining Responsibility

(FAR 9.1)

FAR 9.103 mandates that contracts be awarded only to responsible prospective contractors. The agency contracting officer is responsible for determining that the vendor chosen for contract award is qualified to perform work for the government and capable of doing so. This responsibility determination requirement goes hand in hand with the determination that the price offered is fair and reasonable.

The determination of responsibility must be based on relevant, factual information, as required by regulation, and on sound business judgment reached in good faith. If the contracting officer does not ground his or her judgment of responsibility in fact, a contractor determined to be non-responsible will surely file a protest. However, the Government Accountability Office (GAO) has repeatedly said that contracting officers have broad discretion in exercising sound business judgment when determining responsibility. Thus, GAO rarely sustains non-responsibility protests, unless the protester can demonstrate that the contracting officer had no reasonable basis for the determination or that he or she acted in bad faith.

This chapter is intended to help acquisition professionals understand the purpose of responsibility determination, the information that is used to make the determination, and the responsibility standards contractors must meet.

DETERMINING PROSPECTIVE CONTRACTORS' RESPONSIBILITY

Although the FAR does not require a written responsibility determination for prospective contractors when the contractor is found to be responsible, most agencies do require a written determination. Some agencies require the determination to be included in the price negotiation memorandum, and others require a separate standalone document to be prepared. Regardless, the signing of a contract by the contracting officer constitutes a determination that the prospective contractor is responsible.

In accordance with FAR 9.102(b), the determination of responsibility does *not* apply to proposed contracts with:

(1) Foreign, State, or local governments;
(2) Other U.S. Government agencies or their instrumentalities; or
(3) Agencies for the blind or other severely handicapped (see Subpart 8.7).

The contracting officer is responsible for obtaining sufficient information on the qualifications of the prospective contractor and using discretion in the assessment of the information. The objective is to determine whether the vendor can complete the contract work for the government in a timely and satisfactory manner. In doing so, the prospective contractor's past performance must be taken into consideration. Other sources of information that may be used include:

- ◆ The contractor's record and experience data, including information from knowledgeable personnel from contracting offices within and outside the agency

- ◆ Information submitted with the vendor's proposal or bid

- ◆ Information from the General Services Administration's (GSA) website, Excluded Parties List System, at https://www.epls.gov.

If the information obtained is inadequate to make a determination, the contracting officer may perform a preaward survey or seek information from other sources, such as subcontractors, financial institutions, business and trade associations, and both federal and state government agencies. Preaward surveys are not recommended for acquisitions below the simplified acquisition threshold or for commercial items.

A written determination is required by FAR 9.105-2(1) when a prospective contractor is found to be non-responsible. The contracting officer must prepare the determination of non-responsibility, including the reasons the contractor was deemed non-responsible, and sign it.

STANDARDS FOR PROSPECTIVE CONTRACTORS

All prospective contractors must be able to meet responsibility standards before they can be determined to be responsible.

General Standards

A contractor must meet seven general standards, provided in FAR 9.104-1, to be deemed responsible. It must have:

- The necessary financial resources or the ability to obtain them
- The ability to comply with the delivery or performance schedule
- A satisfactory record of performance
- A satisfactory record of integrity and business ethics
- The necessary organizational experience, accounting and operational controls, and technical skills, or the ability to obtain them
- The necessary equipment and facilities or the ability to obtain them

- ◆ The qualifications and eligibility to receive an award under applicable laws and regulations.

Definitive Responsibility Standards

An agency may include definitive responsibility standards in a solicitation when it wishes to measure the ability of a prospective contractor to perform the contract work. However, these standards must be specific and objective, and they must also be identified in qualitative or quantitative terms. The solicitation must include a provision that informs vendors that the prospective contractor will be required to demonstrate that it will comply with these standards as a precondition to receiving the contract award. If definitive responsibility standards are specified in the solicitation, the contracting officer must take them into consideration when making a responsibility determination. If they are not taken into consideration by the contracting officer, an unsuccessful vendor will likely file a protest challenging the responsibility determination.

In October 2007, such a protest was filed by T. F. Boyle Transportation, Inc., with GAO (B-310708 and B-310708.2, January 29, 2008). The company challenged a Department of Energy (DOE) contracting officer's determination of responsibility in the award of a contract to Visionary Solutions, LLC. T. F. Boyle Transportation alleged that because Visionary Solutions was not able to fulfill the requirement for the Motor Carrier Evaluation Program audit, it had been improperly determined to be a responsible contractor.

The solicitation initially had informed vendors that the vendor selected for award would be required to pass the motor carrier audit as a precondition to receiving the award. The vendors were informed the audit was to be conducted by DOE and would cover all facets of a carrier's business operations. DOE would also review records and equipment. Later, before the due date for proposals, an amendment to the solicitation that deleted the requirement to pass the motor carrier audit was issued.

The protest was denied in January 2008 by GAO, which determined that the provision in the solicitation requiring the prospective contractor to demonstrate its ability to pass the audit did not constitute a definitive responsibility criterion because it did not contain specific and objective standards. Stating that a prospective contractor must possess a specific number of years of experience in a certain type of work (for example, ten years of experience in transporting nuclear waste) *does* constitute a definitive responsibility criterion. But based on the denial of this protest, we see that merely asking a prospective contractor to demonstrate its capability by passing an audit does not set a specific and objective standard.

CHAPTER 15

Reviewing the Award Document

(FAR 4.8, 33.102, 37.103, and 37.104)

The FAR does not provide instructions on legal reviews for award documents, but it does provide examples of records that should be maintained in the agency contract files (FAR 4.803, Contents of Contract Files). The 24th example is "required approvals of award and evidence of legal review." Some agencies, however, do not submit award documents to their legal office for review. An acquisition audit performed on 49 contract files by an agency inspector general reported that many of the files contained inadequate legal reviews or none at all.

Having legal counsel review award documents for legal sufficiency is even more important than obtaining legal review for a solicitation. Some agencies may decide to award a contract without legal review to meet a deadline or because the legal office is unable to provide timely reviews. But acquisition professionals must make sure award documents are submitted for legal review. The review is essential: It ensures that the contract is in compliance with applicable acquisition laws, regulations, executive orders, and government policies and that it is legally binding and enforceable.

REVIEW BY THE ACQUISITION TEAM

Before the legal sufficiency review, the contract document should be reviewed by several acquisition team members to make sure that all of the technical and administrative terms and conditions within are complete and accurate. These team members include:

- Designated government officials from the program office that requested the acquisition, if the contracting officer deems necessary

- Agency officials above the contracting officer, when required by agency policy or determined to be necessary by the contracting officer.

REVIEW BY THE LEGAL OFFICE

In most agencies, the office of legal counsel is responsible for legal sufficiency reviews of acquisition award documents. Legal counsel assess the documents from the standpoint of legal standards rather than technical sufficiency. They may at times review the entire contract file, including all technical information, but usually only for large, complex contracts.

Before award, most technically complex proposed contracts above the simplified acquisition threshold of $150,000 are submitted to the acquisition legal office for legal sufficiency review. For legal counsel to fully understand the proposed contract, it is necessary to submit, at a minimum, the following materials in addition to the award document:

- All correspondence with the successful vendor

- The prenegotiation memorandum

- The price negotiation memorandum

- The successful vendor's proposal

- Any audits or waivers of audits

- The independent government cost estimate

- The summary report of the technical evaluation.

The purpose of the legal sufficiency review is to determine whether a contract is *legally sufficient*. Legal counsel review the document to ensure that:

- The government has the authority to enter into the contract.

- The contract is in compliance with applicable acquisition laws, regulations, executive orders, and agency policies.

- The language in the contract is sufficient to create a legally binding obligation and is legally sufficient. To be legally sufficient, all applicable contract requirements must be substantially satisfied, which includes compliance with laws, rules, and regulations; executive orders; and agency policies.

- The contract accurately reflects the terms and conditions negotiated by the government and contractor.

- The contractual obligations of the contractor and government are clear and identified with certainty.

- The contract will be executed by a person who has been delegated the authority to enter into a contract.

- Specific contract provisions that protect the government are included in the contract, such as the dispute resolution and hold-harmless provisions and other applicable provisions that protect the government.

- All documents attached to the contract are identified properly and are made a part of the contract.

- The descriptions of supplies or services are clear and concise.

- The period of performance or duration of the contract is identified.

- ◆ There are no ambiguous words or phrases in the contract.

- ◆ The total dollar amount of the contract is identified in the contract.

Legal counsel sometimes provide recommendations on ways the contract document can be improved and may suggest usage of more concise and clear words or phrases. Contracts that are not found to be legally sufficient are returned to the acquisition office with noted deficiencies for correction. When the deficiencies are corrected, the contract may be resubmitted to legal counsel for a second review.

AVAILABILITY AND SUFFICIENCY OF CONTRACT FUNDING

Confirming the availability or sufficiency of contract funding is not the responsibility of legal counsel; it is the responsibility of the financial management office within each government agency. These financial management offices are also responsible for providing direction, planning, and oversight of financial policy and procedures, financial reporting, setting accounting policy and procedures, and following up on government audits.

Detailed financial requirements, including those for contract funding, are provided in handbooks developed by the various agencies. These handbooks cover accounting, cash management, credit and debt management, inter- and intra-agency acquisitions, and other financial requirements.

Although legal counsel are not responsible for reviewing contract funding, they often review award documents and associated material to ensure that:

- ◆ The appropriated funds are legally available.

- ◆ The correct amount of funding is identified in the contract document.

- A written document from the responsible financial office indicates adequate funds are available for awarding the contract.

- A written document in the contract file indicates that new fiscal year funds will be used if the contract is to be funded on an annual basis.

- The clause at FAR 52.232-18 (Availability of Funds) is included in the contract when funding from the new fiscal year is to be used.

FISCAL APPROPRIATIONS AND THE ANTIDEFICIENCY ACT

Legal counsel sometimes note in their reviews that fiscal appropriations may be obligated only to meet a bona fide need arising in or continuing to exist in the fiscal year for which the appropriation was made. The legal review notes may also state that funds may not be obligated in excess of funds available or in advance of appropriations for the fiscal year. Obligating funds in excess of the amount available or before approval of the relevant federal appropriation constitutes a violation of the Antideficiency Act, per 31 USC 1341(a)(1)(A) and (B), which states that:

> (1) An officer or employee of the United States Government or of the District of Columbia government may not--
> (A) make or authorize an expenditure or obligation exceeding an amount available in an appropriation or fund for the expenditure or obligation;
> (B) involve either government in a contract or obligation for the payment of money before an appropriation is made unless authorized by law.

Violation of the Antideficiency Act is a very serious matter, and care must be taken when obligating funds. Two types of sanctions may be imposed on employees who violate the statute: administrative and penal. An employee may be suspended from duty without pay or removed from office, or fined not more than $5,000, imprisoned for not more than two years, or both fined and imprisoned.

COMPLIANCE WITH THE ESSENTIAL ELEMENTS OF A CONTRACT

Upon successful completion of the legal sufficiency review and other necessary reviews, the proposed contract is ready to be signed by the contracting officer and the vendor. Once the contract has been deemed legally sufficient and signed by both parties, the document is in compliance with the following four essential elements of a contract:

- **Agreement:** Both the vendor and government have expressed a mutual and common purpose.

- **Consideration:** The offer has been determined to be legally beneficial to the government.

- **Capacity:** Both the vendor and government are legally capable of entering into a contract.

- **Legality of purpose:** The contract is for a legal purpose and will accomplish a specific goal within the federal government.

FAR GUIDANCE ON LEGAL REVIEW

Because acquisition regulations for all agencies are indexed to FAR 4.803, which recommends that certain documents, including evidence of legal review, be placed in the contract file, it is apparent that legal reviews must be made a part of the acquisition process, even if the agency regulation itself does not provide guidance on legal reviews.

All 15 federal agencies identified in Exhibit 11-1 at the end of Chapter 11 have their own agency acquisition regulations that implement and supplement the FAR. As indicated in that chapter, acquisition regulations for most agencies include information on each agency's acquisition review process and the types of acquisition transactions that must be reviewed. If included in the agency's regulation, the legal sufficiency review requirement for award documents will most likely appear in the section that is indexed to FAR part 4, Administrative Matters.

In addition, most federal agencies have internal policies that provide legal review standards for award documents. These policies and procedures can be found in the agency's office of the procurement executive.

DOCUMENTS SUBMITTED FOR LEGAL REVIEW

These acquisition documents and related transactions are normally submitted to the responsible legal office for legal sufficiency review:

- Solicitations
- Award documents
- Contract award documentation
- Modifications to contracts, if required by agency policy
- Ratifications of unauthorized commitments
- Contract claims against the federal government
- Contract terminations
- Interagency agreements
- License agreements
- Novation (transfer of contractor assets) and change-of-name agreements in accordance with FAR 42.12
- Acquisition protests, disputes, and appeals
- Patents, data, and copyrights
- Other acquisition transactions that have been determined by the contracting officer to be vulnerable (i.e., weak in meeting legal standards, liable to protest, or open to protest).

CHAPTER 16

Announcing Contract Awards

(FAR 5.303)

As required by regulation, federal agencies must announce all contract awards of $3.5 million or above to the public, unless agency acquisition regulations mandate a different threshold. The FAR requires all federal agencies to make public announcements regarding their contract awards by 5:00 p.m. Washington, D.C., time on the day of the award. The FAR does not require agencies to notify members of Congress when contracts are awarded in their jurisdictions, but agencies typically want to involve congresspeople in the contract award process. Notifying them is a courtesy. Public announcements and notifications to Congress help keep the federal acquisition system transparent to taxpayers. This transparency is essential to maintaining public trust.

NOTIFICATION THRESHOLDS FOR CONTRACT AWARDS

Most agencies have policies and procedures on the dollar thresholds for making public announcements and notifying members of Congress about contract awards.

Threshold for Public Announcement

FAR 5.303(a) states the following on public announcements of contract awards:

> (a) Public announcement. Contracting officers shall make information available on awards over $3.5 million (unless another dollar

amount is specified in agency acquisition regulations) in sufficient time for the agency concerned to announce it by 5 p.m. Washington, DC, time on the day of award. Agencies shall not release information on awards before the public release time of 5 p.m. Washington, DC time. Contracts excluded from this reporting requirement include—

(1) Those placed with the Small Business Administration under Section 8(a) of the Small Business Act;

(2) Those placed with foreign firms when the place of delivery or performance is outside the United States and its outlying areas; and

(3) Those for which synopsis was exempted under 5.202(a)(1).

Some agencies have established lower or higher thresholds than the threshold required by the FAR for announcement to the public. Some agency thresholds are as low as $250,000, and some are as high as $10 million. For example, the threshold for making a public announcement of contract award for the Department of State is $10 million; for the Department of Defense, it is $5.5 million.

Threshold for Notifying Members of Congress

Because the FAR does not require that Congress be notified of contract awards, agencies that require congressional notification have established various notification thresholds.

For example, the Department of the Interior has established $500,000 as its threshold for notifying members of Congress; the Department of Homeland Security, $1 million. The Department of Defense does not require notification of awards to members of Congress.

An agency's notification threshold can be found in its acquisition regulation, viewable online, under the heading "Publicizing Contract Actions."

PUBLIC ANNOUNCEMENT OF CONTRACT AWARDS

Public announcements are nationwide broadcasts made to the public primarily through newspapers. Federal agencies may also announce contract awards to the local news media. Local announcements regarding contract awards over the simplified acquisition threshold must specify the contracting method used, the number of offers received, and the basis of selection, per FAR 5.303(b):

> For awards after sealed bidding, a statement that the contract was awarded after competition by sealed bidding, the number of offers solicited and received, and the basis for selection (e.g., the lowest responsible bidder); or

> For awards after negotiation, the information prescribed by 15.503(b), and after competitive negotiation (either price or design competition), a statement to this effect, and in general terms the basis for selection.

NOTIFYING MEMBERS OF CONGRESS OF CONTRACT AWARDS

Although the FAR does not require federal agencies to notify members of Congress about contract awards, *agencies do notify the relevant congresspeople* in advance of the agency's public announcement of the award *when a contract will be performed in their state or district.* Federal agencies are aware that members of Congress are accountable to their constituents and have a great deal of interest in the economic benefits of contracts awarded to vendors and organizations located in their jurisdictions. Agencies notify members of Congress early to give them an opportunity to make the initial public announcement of contract awards made in their jurisdictions.

Many agencies have internal policies and procedures for notifying members of Congress. Their notification processes and dollar thresholds for notifying members of Congress vary because they are based on each agency's appropriated funds and need for supplies and services. Small, independent agencies have much smaller appropriations, and they award fewer contracts and lower-cost contracts than do larger agencies. Thus, many smaller agencies have lower dollar thresholds than do larger agencies for notifying members of Congress.

Unless otherwise noted in agency policy, the acquisition office making the award sends a preaward notification to the agency's head of the contracting activity or a senior government official who has been designated to receive the notification. This notification may be sent by electronic mail or facsimile, or it can be hand-carried. It must be delivered at least 24 hours before members of Congress or the vendor who was awarded the contract are notified.

If there are no issues to prevent making the award, either the responsible contracting officer or a designated agency official then notify the appropriate congressional representative or senator. Some agencies require their legislative affairs office or office of legal counsel to take on the responsibility of notifying members of Congress.

The award information must be released specifically to the representative or senator in whose state and district the contract work is to be performed. Notification to members of Congress must be in writing and should provide, at a minimum, the following information:

- ♦ Proposed award date
- ♦ Contractor's name and address
- ♦ The size of the contractor's business
- ♦ Contractor's county and congressional district
- ♦ Contractor's point of contact
- ♦ Geographic location of contract performance
- ♦ Description of the contracted work
- ♦ Dollar amount of the contract for the base year and all option periods.

Once the congressional notification is completed, the vendor that received the award must be notified, preferably by electronic means and then followed by a written notification. Federal agencies rarely release information on contract awards before notifying members of Congress, but sometimes that information is leaked to the public before the notification reaches Congress. To avoid leaks or early release of this information, it is imperative that all employees who participated in the acquisition, as well as the successful vendor, be instructed not to release any information on the award until notified by the contracting officer.

When an unsuccessful vendor submits a protest regarding a contract award after a congressional notification has been issued, the representatives and senators notified of the award must also be notified of the protest immediately. Notification of the protest to members of Congress and agency officials must made be in writing and must state the reason for the protest.

CHAPTER 17

Notifying and Debriefing Unsuccessful Vendors

(FAR 15.306(c)(3), 5.5)

Notifications and debriefings are very important to competing vendors. When an unsuccessful vendor is notified that it is no longer in the competition, it can stop all activities for that acquisition and can then devote its financial and human resources to other business opportunities. If a vendor chooses to be debriefed, it can find out why it was eliminated from the competitive process. Debriefings usually let vendors know the ways in which they must improve. A good debriefing will help a vendor succeed in future competitions and improves the full and open competition process for the government.

Preaward notices are required by FAR 15.503(a), and postaward notices are required by 41 USC 253b(c) and 10 USC 2305(b)(5), as implemented in FAR 15.503(b) (Notification to Unsuccessful Offerors). Preaward debriefings are permitted by 41 USC 253b(f–h) and 10 USC 2305(b)(6)(A) as implemented in FAR 15.505, and, when requested, postaward debriefings are required by 41 USC 253b(e) and 10 USC 2305(b)(5), as implemented in FAR 15.506. Debriefings must be requested in writing by unsuccessful vendors.

WHEN NOTIFICATION AND DEBRIEFING ARE NOT REQUIRED

The FAR does not require federal agencies to issue preaward and postaward notices or debriefings to unsuccessful vendors when using the sealed bidding method of contracting or when purchasing commercial items. Preaward notices are not required when using the simplified acquisition procedures, but postaward notices are required when requested by unsuccessful vendors. Regulation also does not require preaward or postaward notices and debriefings when using contracts under the GSA's Federal Supply Schedule Program. The agency contracting officer has sole discretion regarding the notification and debriefing of GSA schedule vendors.

Many vendors have complained in public newsletters and at various conferences that the federal government does not notify them when they compete for a contract under the Federal Supply Schedule Program and do not receive the contract award. To counter these complaints, it would make good business sense for the responsible acquisition office to tell unsuccessful vendors in writing the reasons they did not receive the award. This would help the vendors improve their acquisition strategies and would improve the government's competitive process.

Because price is the determining factor in most Federal Supply Schedule contracts, notifying unsuccessful vendors would require only a brief form letter or an email. Sending brief messages to these vendors should not increase the workload or expenses of the acquiring organization.

NOTIFYING VENDORS UNDER THE NEGOTIATED METHOD

When contracting by negotiation, the government is required to notify and debrief vendors that were unsuccessful in obtaining a contract award. FAR 15.505(c) requires debriefings for successful and unsuccessful vendors to be done orally or in writing, or by any other method acceptable to the contracting officer. However, most agencies provide oral debriefings, which allow all questions and concerns to be addressed in one session. Also, face-to-face meetings foster more personable relationships between agencies and vendors.

Preaward Notices

Per FAR 15.503(a)(1), the contracting officer must issue a written preaward notice to each vendor whose proposal was excluded from the competitive range. This notice lets unsuccessful vendors know early in the acquisition stage that they are no longer in the competition for a contract award. These vendors, who have spent large amounts of money trying to win the contract, can then direct their financial resources to other business opportunities.

This preaward notification must be issued as soon as the evaluation team and contracting officer decide to exclude the vendors that have no chance of being selected for award. At a minimum, unsuccessful vendors must be told:

- ◆ The basis of the government's determination to exclude the vendor from further competition

- ◆ That the government does not intend to consider a proposal revision from the vendor

- ◆ That the vendor may request a debriefing before the government makes a contract award.

It is imperative that the preaward notice make clear that vendors must request a debriefing within three days after receiving the preaward notice from the government.

Per FAR 15.503(a)(2), the contracting officer is required to issue preaward notices to unsuccessful vendors that competed for a contract under the following small business programs:

- ◆ Set-asides for small business (FAR 19.5)

- ◆ Small disadvantaged business participation (FAR 19.11)

- Historically underutilized business zone (HUBZone) (FAR 19.1305 or 19.1307)

- Service-disabled veteran-owned small business procurement (FAR 19.1405).

When necessary, the preaward notice must be issued to both the vendor and Small Business Administration. The preaward notice must be issued before the contract is awarded but after negotiations have been completed and a determination of responsibility has been made.

Postaward Notices

The acquisition statutes at 41 USC 253b(d)(3) and 10 USC 2305(b)(4) (C) require agencies to award a contract with reasonable promptness to the vendor whose proposal is most advantageous to the government. Per FAR 15.503(b), which implements 41 USC 253b(e) and 10 USC 2305(b)(5), once the technical and price evaluations have been completed and the contract has been awarded, the contracting officer must notify in writing each vendor whose proposal was in the competitive range but was not selected for award. Postaward notices must also be issued upon request to unsuccessful vendors when using the simplified acquisition procedures. The written notice must be issued within three days after contract award.

A postaward notice explains the reasons a particular vendor was not selected. It also states the name of the vendor selected because unsuccessful vendors may seek subcontracting opportunities with the winning vendor. Finally, the notice must inform the vendor that it may request a debriefing within three days after receiving the notice. The postaward notice must include at a minimum, the following information:

- The number of vendors that submitted proposals

- The number of proposals received

- A brief explanation of why the vendor did not receive the award

- The name and address of the vendor that received the award

- The supplies or services purchased and the total contract price of the award

- A brief, general explanation of why the winning vendor's proposal was selected.

Most agencies release only the total price of the contract award, but a listing of the items and quantities ordered can be released if desired. Unit prices of the items may *not* be released if exempt from release under the Freedom of Information Act (5 USC 552(b)).

Any information provided in a proposal that is privileged or confidential between the proposing vendor and the government may *not* be released to unsuccessful vendors or to the public. It is imperative that vendors be told what information the government intends to release to the public before it is released. Most vendors will cooperate regarding the release of their information, but some will not; they consider their entire technical and price proposals to be privileged or confidential. Acquisition laws and regulations permit the disclosure of certain information from technical and price proposals. Assistance from the agency legal counsel should be sought when vendors do not agree to the disclosure of their technical or price information.

A sample letter to an unsuccessful vendor that was in the competitive range but was not selected for the award of a government contract appears in Exhibit 17-1. This sample can be modified to fit actual acquisition actions.

EXHIBIT 17-1: Sample Letter to an Unsuccessful Vendor

Insert name and address of unsuccessful vendor. Send via fax and registered mail.

Subject: Request for quotations (RFQ) or request for proposals (RFP) number

_____

Dear _____:

The government has completed its evaluation of the proposals submitted in response to solicitation number *(insert RFQ or RFP number)*. After evaluating your proposal, we have determined that it did not represent the best value to the government.

The government received and evaluated a total of *(insert number)* proposals. The evaluation was performed in accordance with the technical and price criteria identified in the *(RFQ or RFP)*. You did not receive the award because your offer did not provide an overall best value to the government, technical evaluation criteria and cost considered.

The contract for the amount of *(dollar amount)* for a one-year period with four option years has been awarded to:

(Insert name and address of vendor that received the contract award.)

We wish to thank you for participating in the competition and encourage your organization to compete in future acquisitions.

If you desire a debriefing, you must request it in writing within three days from receipt of this notice as required by FAR 15.505. Any request for a debriefing should be addressed to *(name of contracting officer)* and submitted by fax at *(fax number)* or sent to the following mailing address:

(Insert name, address, and point of contact for government acquisition office.)

Sincerely,

_____
Contracting officer's signature

When one unsuccessful vendor protests an award decision, other unsuccessful vendors may decide to help the protestor challenge the decision. To avoid frivolous protests and prevent unsuccessful vendors from taking other negative actions, preaward and postaward notifications should reiterate that the evaluation was based on the criteria specified in the solicitation.

DEBRIEFING VENDORS UNDER THE NEGOTIATED METHOD

An unsuccessful vendor that does not submit a timely debriefing request during the preaward or postaward phases need not be given a debriefing, per FAR 15.505(a)(3). Although the contracting officer is required to debrief unsuccessful vendors as soon as possible, he or she may refuse to provide a debriefing when it is determined that doing so is not in the best interest of the government.

The contracting officer may also delay a preaward debriefing until after the contract is awarded but must document in the contract file why it was not promptly held. When a preaward debriefing is delayed, the contracting officer must provide the debriefing no later than the postaward debriefings. If an unsuccessful vendor submits a protest regarding a delayed preaward debriefing to the agency or the Government Accountability Office (GAO), it will most likely be denied because debriefings are entirely within the discretion of the contracting officer.

Preaward Debriefings

Preaward debriefings should be conducted by the contracting officer responsible for awarding the contract. As required by FAR 15.505(e), a preaward debriefing must include, at a minimum, the following:

- ◆ A listing of significant elements found in the vendor's proposal

- ◆ The reason for eliminating the vendor from further competition

- ◆ Reasonable responses to questions posed by vendors on whether selection procedures provided in the solicitation and other applicable rules and regulations were followed.

The government may not disclose certain information to vendors that were excluded from the competitive range in the early stage of an acquisition. The statutes at 41 USC 253b(f)(4) and 10 USC 2305(b)(6)

(D) state the following on disclosure of information to unsuccessful vendors during preaward debriefings:

> The debriefing conducted pursuant to this subsection may not disclose the number or identity of other offerors and shall not disclose information about the content, ranking, or evaluation of other offerors' proposals.

The statutory requirement on disclosure of information implemented in FAR 15.505(f) states that the following information may not be disclosed during a preaward debriefing:

- ◆ The number of vendors that competed for the acquisition
- ◆ The names of all unsuccessful vendors
- ◆ The content of proposals submitted by unsuccessful vendors
- ◆ Ranking of all unsuccessful vendors (when ranking is done)
- ◆ Proposal evaluation results for all unsuccessful vendors
- ◆ Information that is exempt from release under the Freedom of Information Act, including:
  - › Trade secrets
  - › Privileged or confidential information
  - › Commercial and financial information
  - › The identity of the person or people who provided information on the past performance of an unsuccessful vendor.

It is very important not to disclose certain information to unsuccessful vendors, because doing so can harm the remaining competing vendors. Vendor information that is exempt from disclosure under the Freedom of Information Act must not be disclosed to any vendor during a debriefing. Exemption 4 of the Freedom of Information Act prohibits disclosure of trade secrets, commercial or financial information obtained from a person, and information that is considered to be privileged or confidential. Information in proposals received from competing vendors is often marked as privileged or confidential, but it may not really be privileged or confidential. Therefore, it is advisable to seek assistance from the agency legal counsel before disclosing any information that is considered to be privileged or confidential by vendors, or when pieces of information are exempted from disclosure by law or regulation.

A good, comprehensive preaward debriefing makes clear to vendors the reasons they were removed from the competition and helps them understand how to improve their proposals in the future. In addition to providing information on weaknesses and deficiencies, contracting officers often highlight the strong points of a vendor's proposal.

A preaward debriefing must be documented and filed in the contract file to serve as background information in support of the contract award decision.

Vendors excluded from the competitive range or excluded from further competition for other reasons before contract award may elect a postaward debriefing instead of a preaward debriefing. Although the FAR is silent on this, it is reasonable to assume that such a request may be accepted by the contracting officer. Contracting officers have the authority to delay preaward debriefings when doing so is in the best interest of the government. They are also likely to have a smaller workload during the postaward stage of an acquisition.

Postaward Debriefings

When requested, postaward debriefings must be provided to vendors that were in the competitive range but did not receive the contract award. A request for a postaward debriefing must be submitted in writing within three days of receiving a postaward notification. The contracting officer should provide the debriefing within five days from receipt of a written request. Vendors that requested postaward debriefings at the time they received a preaward notification and vendors whose preaward debriefings were delayed also must be debriefed during this time period.

Contracting officers are not mandated by acquisition regulation to perform the debriefing within five days from receipt of a request but are encouraged to do so to the maximum extent practicable. The statutory requirement for postaward debriefing provided in 41 USC 253b(e) and 10 USC 2305(b)(5), as implemented in FAR 15.506(a)(1) and (2), provides guidance on the debriefing:

> (a)(1) An offeror, upon its written request received by the agency within 3 days after the date on which that offeror has received notification of contract award in accordance with 15.503(b), shall be debriefed and furnished the basis for the selection decision and contract award.
>
> (2) To the maximum extent practicable, the debriefing should occur within 5 days after receipt of the written request. Offerors that requested a postaward debriefing in lieu of a preaward debriefing, or whose debriefing was delayed for compelling reasons beyond contract award, also should be debriefed within this time period.

The contracting officer may allow delayed postaward or preaward debriefings for unsuccessful vendors who submit a request to delay. However, the request for a delayed debriefing must be submitted within three days.

The contracting officer should lead the debriefing. Evaluation team members provide technical support and should be ready to address technical weaknesses and deficiencies found in the proposal. When necessary, a price analyst and legal advisor can be asked to offer additional support. FAR 15.506(d) requires the government debriefing team to provide, at a minimum, the following information to each unsuccessful vendor at its postaward debriefing session:

- ◆ Significant weaknesses or deficient factors and subfactors found in the vendor's proposal
- ◆ The evaluated cost or price and technical rating, when applicable, of successful and unsuccessful proposals, and past performance information on unsuccessful vendors.

- ◆ Overall ranking of all vendors (if ranking was developed)

- ◆ A summary of the rationale for the contract award

- ◆ Reasonable responses to questions posed by vendors on whether selection procedures provided in the solicitation and other applicable rules and regulations were followed.

FAR 15.306(d)(3) states that the contracting officer is not required to discuss every part of the proposal that could be improved. Also, FAR 15.306(e)(3) states that the contracting officer may inform a competing vendor that its costs are too high or low or are not as competitive as those of other competing vendors. When a vendor is told that its costs are not as competitive as those that were offered by other vendors, the contracting officer must provide the results of the cost or price analysis that supports this judgment.

A detailed debriefing will help an unsuccessful vendor develop better proposals in the future. The debriefing should provide useful, reasonable information that vendors can use when preparing future proposals. As for preaward debriefings, it is important to address the strong points of a vendor's proposal, not just its weaknesses and deficiencies. A debriefing that includes a good explanation of the evaluation process, the government's assessment of the vendor's proposal relative to the evaluation criteria, and the rationale for not selecting the vendor for award will give the vendor a general understanding of the award decision. It will also instill confidence in the vendor that its proposal and its competitors were evaluated fairly.

The government may not release certain information to unsuccessful vendors during postaward debriefing if doing so could harm other vendors that competed in the acquisition. Proposals submitted in response to a competitive solicitation must never be made available to anyone, in accordance with the Freedom of Information Act. However, proposals may be released to the public if the entire proposal or a large portion of it was made a part of the award document. Making the entire proposal a part of the contract is not recommended.

As required for preaward debriefings, information that is confidential or proprietary and information exempt from disclosure under the Freedom of Information Act may not be disclosed to any of the vendors during the postaward debriefing. FAR 15.506(e) prohibits the disclosure of the following types of information during a postaward debriefing:

- ◆ A point-by-point comparison of proposals submitted by other vendors who competed in the acquisition

- ◆ Any proposal received by the government under the full and open competition method of contracting, unless it has been made a part of the contract

- ◆ Any dispute resolution information that is exempt under the Freedom of Information Act

- ◆ Information that is exempt from release under the Freedom of Information Act, including:

    - ➤ Trade secrets

    - ➤ Privileged or confidential information

    - ➤ Commercial and financial information

    - ➤ The identity of the person or people who provided information on the past performance of an unsuccessful vendor.

Protests Filed after a Debriefing

When an unsuccessful vendor believes that the government did not clearly explain in its debriefing why the vendor was not selected for the contract award, the vendor may file a protest with the agency contracting officer or with GAO, as permitted by regulation. A protest filed after award must be filed by an *interested party*, meaning a competing vendor that has a direct economic interest in the acquisition and has a reasonable chance of receiving the award if the protest is sustained.

Protests submitted to an agency must be filed within ten days after contract award or within five days after the preaward or postaward debriefings. When a protest is filed with an agency, the contracting officer must immediately notify the contractor and ask that work be suspended. All vendors that were asked to submit final revised proposals prior to award but did not receive the award must also be notified of the protest. Agencies are strongly encouraged to settle agency protests within 35 days.

Protests submitted to GAO must also be filed within ten days after contract award or within five days after the preaward or postaward debriefings. When a vendor files a protest with GAO, GAO notifies the agency contracting officer within one day of receipt of the protest. Upon receiving the protest notification, the agency contracting officer must suspend contract performance or terminate the contract that was awarded. Exhibit 17-2 is a sample stop work letter to the winning vendor. The contractor and all vendors that were asked to submit final revised proposals prior to award must be notified of the protest and whether performance will stop or continue during the protest period.

EXHIBIT 17-2: Sample Letter to a Contractor Lifting a Stop Work Request

(Insert name and address of contractor.)

Dear _____ :

You were notified on *(date and year)* that *(protesting company's name)* and *(name of second protestor if applicable)* protested the *(name of contract)* awarded to your company on *(date of award)*. You were also notified by telephone on *(date)* to stop work until further notice. This telephone notification was followed up with a written request on *(date)*.

In accordance with the Federal Acquisition Regulation at 33.104(c)(2), a request to continue the performance of contract number _____ was submitted to the head of the contracting activity on *(date)* for review and approval. The request to continue performance was approved on *(date)*, and the stop work request is hereby lifted. You are asked to start performance under this contract on *(date)*.

If you have questions, please call me at *(telephone number)*.

Sincerely,

_____
Contracting officer's signature

Performance may be continued only if it is authorized by the head of the contracting activity when doing so is in the best interest of the government or if it is for an urgent and compelling reason. Per FAR 1.7, when an agency decides to continue performance, the head of the contracting activity must prepare a determination and findings (D&F), written approval to continue contract performance. A D&F is usually prepared for a single contract action, but it may be prepared for classes of contract actions, unless prohibited by statute or regulation. See Exhibit 17-3 for a sample D&F.

EXHIBIT 17-3: Sample Determination and Findings to Continue Contract Performance

Department of *(agency name)*
(Insert city, state, and ZIP Code)

Determination and findings for contract number _____

Authority to Continue Contract Performance

On *(date)*, the contracting officer of *(name of agency or organization)* was notified of a protest related to the award of contract number _____ made by *(name of protestor)*. The contract was signed on *(date award was signed)*, and vendors were notified by a letter dated *(date)*. The contractor, *(name of contractor)*, began operations on *(date)*, and was requested to stop work on *(date)*.

In accordance with the Federal Acquisition Regulation at 33.104(c)(2), it is my determination as the head of the contracting activity that the suspension of the *(name of contract)* contract will result in immediate injury to the interests of the United States and that continuing contract performance is critical to the mission of the *(name of agency or organization)* for the following reasons:

Findings

(Provide brief but comprehensive justification that supports the continuation of the contract that has been protested.)

Determination

In accordance with FAR 33.104(c)(2)(i), I have determined that it is in the best interest of the United States to continue the performance of the *(name of contract)* contract until the Government Accountability Office has made a recommendation on the protest of the award. Therefore, the contractor, *(insert name and complete address)*, is hereby authorized to continue performance.

_____   _____
Head of the contracting activity's signature   Date

The contractor may not be authorized to continue performance until GAO has received the agency's justification. When there is an urgent and compelling reason to continue contract performance, the head of the contracting activity does not have to await a GAO decision. When the decision to continue contract performance has been justified and approved, the contractor and all vendors asked to submit final revised proposals prior to award must be notified in writing. See Exhibit 17-4 for a sample letter to an unsuccessful vendor in the competitive range on the decision to continue contract performance. Notifications to the contractor and vendors regarding the protest and the government's decision to continue performance may be made by telephone but must be followed up in writing, either by facsimile or by regular mail.

EXHIBIT 17-4: Sample Letter to an Unsuccessful Vendor on Continuing Contract Performance

(Insert name and address of contractor.)

Dear _____:

In accordance with the Federal Acquisition Regulation at 33.104(d), you are hereby notified that a decision has been made to continue performance of contract number _____ to provide *(type of supplies or services)*.

(Name of contractor) was notified on *(date)* that *(name of protestor)* and *(name of second protestor if applicable)* protested the contract awarded to *(name of contractor)* on *(date)*. The company was notified on *(date)* to stop work until further notice. In accordance with FAR 33.104(c)(2), the request to continue performance for the contract has been approved by the head of the contracting activity. The stop work request has been lifted, and *(name of contractor)* has been asked to continue performance.

Sincerely,

_____
Contracting officer's signature

GAO will issue a decision within 100 days from the day the protest was filed or within 65 days under an expedited schedule referred to as the *express option*. The express option may be requested by the interested party, or GAO may decide on its own that the protest can be resolved under the express option.

The acquisition protest process is described in a GAO booklet, *Bid Protests at GAO: A Descriptive Guide.* It is available online at http://www.gao.gov/decisions/bidpro/bid/d09417sp.pdf.

Protests Filed after an Award

A unsuccessful vendor may file a protest based on its belief that because its technical or cost information was not addressed in its debriefing, the agency failed to engage in meaningful discussion.

Such a protest was filed with GAO by Integrated Concepts & Research Corporation (B-309803, October 15, 2007). The company protested the award of a contract to Concurrent Technologies Corporation (CTC) for research and development, test, and evaluation support for the U.S. Air Force's Advanced Power Technology Office. Integrated Concepts (ICRC) said that the Air Force did not hold meaningful discussions with the company. ICRC argued that the Air Force should have informed the company that its proposed costs were so much higher than CTC's that it had no chance of receiving the award. ICRC asserted that the Air Force did not make clear that its costs were a deficiency. ICRC also claimed that the award was tainted by an organizational conflict of interest, but it withdrew that allegation because there was no basis for it.

The comptroller general concluded that the discussions between the Air Force and ICRC were neither misleading nor inadequate, and he further stated that when a vendor's cost is too high in comparison to the competitors' costs, the agency may, but is not required to, inform the vendor during discussions that its costs are not as competitive as those of its competitors. After reviewing the protest, the comptroller general concluded that the Air Force's evaluation was reasonable, and its discussion with the protester was adequate. The protest was denied.

CHAPTER 18

The Federal Supply Schedule Program and Price Reductions

(FAR 8.4, 38.0)

The federal government's use of the Federal Supply Schedule Program has increased considerably within the last ten years. This is because the amount of commercial supplies and services provided by the program has increased and because the program simplifies obtaining commercial items and price discounts and reductions for customers. Despite the program's growing popularity, some agencies still do not take advantage of the price discounts and reductions that are permitted by regulation. This program allows the government to request price discounts and reductions prior to award. Discounts and reductions are normally requested during the evaluation, negotiation, and award phase of the acquisition process.

This chapter explains the Federal Supply Schedule Program and offers guidance on price discounts and reductions offered by schedule vendors. Acquisition professionals are encouraged to become familiar with the program's benefits.

The Federal Supply Service within the General Services Administration (GSA) awards and manages contracts under its Federal Supply Schedule Program, also known as the GSA Schedules Program and Multiple Award Schedule Program. This program simplifies the process for obtaining commercial supplies or services that are commonly used in the open marketplace.

The Department of Veterans Affairs (VA) also has a schedule program for medical supplies. (GSA delegated the VA the responsibility for the acquisition of medical supplies in 1994.) Information on the VA Federal Supply Schedule programs can be found at http://www1 .va.gov/oamm/oa/nac/fsss/index.cfm.

FEDERAL SUPPLY SCHEDULE CONTRACTS

GSA negotiates and awards contracts to responsible commercial vendors that provide supplies and services at discounted commercial prices for given periods of time. Once GSA awards a Federal Supply Schedule (hereafter referred to as Schedule) contract, federal agencies can place orders directly with Schedule contractors, which are responsible for taking orders and delivering the supplies and services.

Schedule contracts for both supplies and services are awarded as indefinite-delivery indefinite-quantity (IDIQ) contracts and are available to all federal agencies worldwide. In accordance with FAR 8.404(a), ordering activities that use the Schedule ordering procedures are not required to seek competition outside the Schedule program. Each contract has a minimum and maximum dollar threshold for ordering that the federal government must honor.

Use of Schedule Contracts by Local and State Governments

In the spring of 2007, GSA began allowing state and local governments to order supplies and services using Schedule contracts, but only to support recovery from major disasters and acts of terrorism. State and local governments were authorized to use Schedule contracts for reasons other than disaster and terrorism support when the president of the United States signed into law the Local Preparedness Acquisition Act (Public Law 110-248) on June 26, 2008. This law authorizes state and local governments to use Schedule contracts for the acquisition of law enforcement and security-related items as well as firefighting and rescue equipment.

By using Schedule contracts, state and local governments can receive the same discounted prices provided to the federal government. These governments will likely save millions of dollars by using Schedule contracts to purchase law enforcement and security-related items.

Schedule Prices Are Fair and Reasonable

The prices listed in Schedule contracts have been negotiated by GSA and have been determined to be fair and reasonable. These prices are comparable to volume prices in the commercial marketplace and are commonly called *most-favored customer prices*. Therefore, the government as the ordering customer is allowed to fulfill its requirements by making best value selections of the supplies or services that meet its needs.

New Protest Requirement for Schedule Contracts

For many years, task or delivery orders issued against IDIQ contracts could not be protested by a vendor that was not successful in receiving an award for a government contract. The debate on protesting IDIQ orders went back and forth for over a decade until fiscal year 2008. The National Defense Authorization Act (P.L. 110-181, 122 Stat. 3) was signed into law on January 28, 2008. Section 843 of the authorization act (Enhanced Competition Requirements for Task and Delivery Order Contracts) opened the door to bid protests for task and delivery orders in excess of $10 million.

The law, which went into effect on May 27, 2008, gives contractors the ability to protest individual task or delivery orders over $10 million. Contractors can place their bid protests with the Government Accountability Office. This new protest requirement will expire three years from the effective date of May 27, 2008, unless extended. FAR

16.505 (a)(9), as revised in FY 2009, permits contractors to protest an order under a task or delivery order contract when the:

- ◆ Scope of the requirement has been increased;
- ◆ Period of performance has been increased; or
- ◆ Maximum value of the contract has been increased; and
- ◆ Orders are valued in excess of $10 million.

Ordering Procedures for Schedule Contracts

Federal agencies do not have to advertise their requirements or seek competition outside the list of vendors identified in Schedule contracts. However, they are required to follow the procedures provided in FAR 8.405 for all orders placed against contracts under the Schedule program. FAR 8.405-1 details ordering procedures for supplies and services that do not require an SOW. Prices for these supplies and services are listed as fixed prices in a Schedule contract. Ordering procedures for services with hourly rates that do require an SOW are provided in FAR 8.405-2. Additional detailed information on the Federal Supply Schedule Program can be found online at www.gsa.gov/schedules.

BLANKET PURCHASE AGREEMENTS

Federal agencies can establish blanket purchase agreements with selected Schedule contractors to fill repetitive needs for supplies or services. A blanket purchase agreement established with a Schedule contractor may not contain terms and conditions that are inconsistent with the Schedule contract used to establish the agreement. Both single and multiple blanket purchase agreements may be established with Schedule contractors that have been determined to offer the best value. (A single blanket purchase agreement is made with only one vendor; a multiple agreement, with two or more vendors.)

Under a single blanket purchase agreement, all authorized users can place their orders directly with the Schedule contractor that is the holder of the agreement. There are no additional requirements to meet or determinations to make. When ordering under multiple blanket purchase agreements, every Schedule contractor that is a holder of the agreement must be given a copy of the government's SOW and the associated evaluation criteria for orders exceeding the micropurchase threshold of $3,000. Upon receipt and evaluation of responses from holders of the agreement, a best-value determination is made, and authorized users are permitted to place their orders with the Schedule contractor that represents the best value.

Using blanket purchase agreements benefits the government in several ways:

- ◆ Administrative costs are reduced.

- ◆ Solicitations do not have to be prepared.

- ◆ The government's requirements need not be publicized.

- ◆ The terms and conditions are already contained in the Schedule contracts against which blanket purchase agreements are established.

- ◆ The ordering, invoicing, and payment processes are simplified.

- ◆ Additional discounts can be obtained through volume purchasing.

- ◆ Individual purchases from Schedule contractors can be eliminated, and all orders can be consolidated under one ordering mechanism.

- ◆ The ordering and delivery processes can be expedited.

- ◆ The milestone schedule for the acquisition can be shortened.

PRICE DISCOUNTS AND REDUCTIONS

Price discounts and reductions may include one-time discounts; reductions from discounted prices; and reductions below the maximum threshold.

One-Time Discounts

Vendors that have contracts under the Schedule program may offer a one-time discount from the established contract prices listed in the Schedule contracts for a specific order. They are not required to pass the same discount to other customers placing orders against the same contract. Schedule contractors can be more competitive if they give higher discounts to one buying customer rather than giving the same (lower) discount to all customers buying the same supplies or services.

Price discounts offered under the Schedule program allow the federal government to take advantage of the flexible pricing practices in the commercial marketplace. They also allow the government to negotiate discounts without having to prepare and negotiate new contracts.

Reductions from Discounted Prices

Under Schedule contracts, supplies or services that serve the same general purpose or function are grouped, and each is assigned a *special item number* (SIN) with an established maximum dollar threshold. This maximum threshold is the point at which it is advantageous for the government to seek a price reduction when acquiring that type of supply or service. Per FAR 8.405-4, federal agencies are required to seek price reductions from the already discounted Schedule prices when their orders exceed the maximum dollar thresholds identified in the contract. They are also advised to seek price reductions, when warranted, for orders under the maximum dollar thresholds.

FAR 8.405-1(d) outlines the ordering procedure for orders exceeding the maximum ordering threshold for supplies and services that do not require an SOW:

> **Orders exceeding the maximum order threshold.** Each schedule contract has a maximum order threshold established on a SIN-by-SIN basis. Although a price reduction may be sought at any time, this threshold represents the point where, given the dollar value of the potential order, the ordering activity shall seek a price reduction.

In addition to following the procedures in paragraph (c) of this section and before placing an order that exceeds the maximum order threshold or establishing a BPA (see 8.405-3), ordering activities shall—

1) Review (except see (c)(2) of this subsection) the pricelists of additional schedule contractors (the GSA Advantage! on-line shopping service can be used to facilitate this review);

(2) Based upon the initial evaluation, seek price reductions from the schedule contractor(s) considered to offer the best value (see 8.404(d)); and

(3) After seeking price reductions (see 8.405-4), place the order with the schedule contractor that provides the best value. If further price reductions are not offered, an order may still be placed.

When the government seeks price reductions for orders above the maximum dollar threshold identified in the Schedule contract, the vendor may do one of three things:

◆ Offer a new, lower price

◆ Offer the current price listed in the Schedule contract

◆ Decline the order within five working days.

The maximum dollar threshold is provided in the terms and conditions of all Schedule contracts. It can usually be found in the section entitled Delivery Schedule. Exhibit 18-1 shows a sample maximum ordering provision that might appear in the terms and conditions of an information technology Schedule contract.

EXHIBIT 18-1: Sample Maximum Ordering Provision

Maximum order

All dollar amounts are exclusive of any discount for prompt payment.

The maximum order value for the following special item numbers (SINs) is $500,000:

Special item number 132-51: Information technology (IT) professional services

---

Reductions below the Maximum Threshold

The government may seek a price reduction for an order under the maximum threshold when doing so is found to be advantageous. Price reductions may be requested for any acquisition between the micropurchase threshold of $3,000 and the maximum dollar threshold specified in the Schedule contract. It is appropriate to request price reductions for items on a Schedule contract if the same items are available in the open marketplace at lower prices, even if the order is below the maximum threshold.

It is also appropriate to seek price reductions when using blanket purchase agreements to purchase supplies that must be kept in stock on a continuous basis or services that are repetitive in nature. Because many repetitive needs are purchased in large volume under blanket purchase agreements, it is not only appropriate but in the best interest of the government to seek price reductions. Schedule contractors sometimes offer additional discounts for frequent and large-volume orders.

PART IV
The Postaward Phase

CHAPTER 19

Nomination, Training, Certification, and Responsibilities of the Contracting Officer's Representative

(FAR 15.5, 27.4, and 31.2)

The last phase of the federal acquisition process is known as the *postaward phase* or *contract administration*. Although contracting officers have the primary responsibility for monitoring contracts during the contract administration phase, they must rely on their designated representatives to assist with the administration of awarded contracts. The main representative for a contracting officer is called the *contracting officer's technical representative* (COTR) or *contracting officer's representative* (COR). These terms are used by the federal government for employees who have been appointed to serve as government representatives during the last phase of the acquisition cycle. For the purposes of this book, the term *COTR* is equivalent to *COR*.

The Office of Federal Procurement Policy (OFPP) has found that COTRs often have unclear roles and responsibilities and have not been properly trained to perform contract oversight. For the government to receive quality supplies or services that are delivered in a timely manner, it is essential for COTRs to have the required training and certification to carry out their contract administration responsibilities. Contracting officers rely on properly trained COTRs to ensure that contractors' performance is adequate and costs are controlled.

NOMINATION AND TRAINING OF THE COTR

The program office that requested the acquisition is responsible for nominating and recommending the person who will serve as the COTR for the contract. COTRs must be federal government employees, unless agency regulation authorizes the use of non-federal employees. When authorized, contractors may act as COTRs, but usually only to perform inspection or testing services under the supervision of the government COTR or contracting officer.

In most agencies, the appointment of the representative that is nominated or recommended by the program office is within the discretion of the contracting officer; although some agencies require the procurement executive or the head of the contracting activity to make the appointment, particularly if a contractor is to be used.

In the current acquisitions environment, OFPP encourages agencies to appoint COTRs based on their technical and management experience. In the past, selection of COTRs was strictly based on their technical expertise. Many COTRs held the position on a temporary basis and usually left the position before a contract was completed. As a result, contract administration lacked consistency.

All agencies are now required to train and certify COTRs before delegating contract administration authority to them. In 2007, OFPP issued a memorandum, *The Federal Acquisition Certification for Contracting Officer Technical Representatives*, which established a structured training program called the Federal Acquisition Certification Program. The program requires all COTRs to be trained and certified, preferably prior to being formally appointed by a contracting officer.

COTR Training Courses

Although the duties and responsibilities of a COTR vary from agency to agency, each COTR must complete 40 hours of training, including acquisition-related and general business management courses, as required by the OFPP Federal Acquisition Certification Program. When a COTR who has not had the required training is nominated and appointed, he or she must start the training program within 90 days of being appointed.

Twenty-two of the required 40 hours of COTR training must cover various professional business and technical competencies, as required by the OFPP. These competencies are listed in Exhibit 19-1 and can also be found on the OFPP website at http://www.fai.gov/pdfs/11-26-COTR-Memo.pdf. The training curriculum suggested by the OFPP includes the courses listed below. Federal agencies are permitted to substitute other types of training courses in place of the OFPP-recommended courses, but they must ensure that the substituted courses cover the essential required competencies listed in Exhibit 19-1.

- ◆ COTR with a Mission Focus (8 continuous learning points (CLPs))
- ◆ Contracting Overview (8 CLPs)
- ◆ Market Research (3 CLPs)
- ◆ Contract Source Selection (1 CLP)
- ◆ Ethics Training for Acquisition, Technology, and Logistics (2 CLPs).

EXHIBIT 19-1: COTR Key Competencies	
Professional business competencies	**Technical competencies**
Oral communication	Understanding COTR duties, responsibilities, and obligations
Decision-making	Effective communication of contract requirements
Teamwork	Effective performance management
Problem solving	Strategic planning
Attention to detail	Detailed evaluation skills
Reasoning	Defining business relationships
Flexibility	Understanding the marketplace
Interpersonal skills	Effective communication
Self-management/ initiative	Defining government requirements in commercial/ noncommercial terms
Integrity/honesty	Effective negotiation skills and effective analytical skills
Planning and evaluating	
Influencing/negotiating	
Writing	
Project management	

Eighteen of the 40 hours of training can be elective courses, agency-specific courses, or courses recommended by the agency official who manages the COTR program.

Upon completing the 40 hours of training, the COTR is certified by the Federal Acquisition Institute. Once trained and certified, the COTR is formally appointed by the contracting officer. He or she is now ready to represent the government and becomes responsible for all technical aspects of the contract work to be performed.

Continuous Learning Points

Once appointed, COTRs are required to maintain their skills through their agency's continuous learning program. To keep skills current and maintain the COTR certification, COTRs must earn 40 CLPs every two years. If a COTR does not do so, his or her certification will expire, and the delegation to serve as a COTR will be revoked. To earn CLPs, the COTR may:

- Take agency-approved training courses

- Participate in professional organizations that award continuing education units

- Participate in formal training programs that award continuing education units

- Take formal academic courses offered by public or private educational institutions.

COTR Training Institutions

Unless agency policy dictates a specific training institution, prospective COTRs may obtain training at any of the following institutions:

- Federal Acquisition Institute

- Defense Acquisition University

- Colleges or universities

- Federal agencies

- Commercial training organizations.

The COTR Nomination and Delegation Memoranda

The program office must notify the contracting officer in writing when a COTR is nominated. The nomination memorandum should:

- List the COTR's qualifications relative to the requirements of the contract

- Detail the COTR's experience in the technical and management areas relevant to the contract

- List all COTR training courses the nominee has taken.

A copy of the training certificate should be attached to the memorandum. Exhibit 19-2 shows a sample COTR nomination memorandum that can be modified to fit any acquisition action.

EXHIBIT 19-2: Sample COTR Nomination Memorandum

MEMORANDUM

To: *(name of contracting officer)*
From: *(name of manager of program office)*
Subject: *(name of COTR nominee)*

(Name of COTR nominee) has been nominated as the COTR for *(name of contract)*. This nomination is based on *(name of COTR nominee)*'s qualifications and experience, both technical and management, and training.

The following information is provided for your review and consideration.

Technical qualifications and experience
Describe type of work performed.

Management experience
Describe types of contracts and other related projects administered.

Required training
List the 22 hours of mandatory training courses and 18 hours of elective training courses taken.

Attachment: certificate of appointment

Once the COTR has been appointed, a delegation memorandum should be issued to the COTR. This memorandum must explain the scope of the COTR's authority and must be signed by both the COTR and the contracting officer. The delegation memorandum to the COTR must, at a minimum:

- ◆ Identify the contract that the COTR will monitor
- ◆ Outline the scope of the COTR's authority
- ◆ Identify the COTR's duties and responsibilities
- ◆ Delineate contract actions the COTR is not authorized to perform.

See Exhibit 19-3 for a sample delegation memorandum.

EXHIBIT 19-3: Sample Delegation Memorandum

MEMORANDUM

To: *(name of contracting officer's technical representative)*
From: *(name of contracting officer)*
Subject: Delegation of authority under contract number _____

As the authorized contracting officer, I hereby designate you as the contracting officer's technical representative (COTR). You are requested to provide assistance in all technical matters that are within the scope of contract number _____, which was awarded to *(name of contractor)* on *(month, day, and year).* This delegation authorizes you to perform the tasks listed under paragraphs 1 and 2 but does not include tasks listed in paragraph 3.

1. Technical matters/directions
List tasks related to technical issues, such as providing technical clarification to the contractor, monitoring and inspecting the contractor's progress, inspecting and approving contract deliverables, and any other technical duties.

2. Nontechnical matters
List tasks such as reviewing and approving contractor invoices, notifying the contracting officer if the contractor fails to make progress, and other matters.

3. Prohibited acquisition actions
List tasks such as modifying or altering any contract terms and conditions, waiving any rights of the government pertaining to the contract, and other proscribed actions.

You are asked to notify the contracting officer in writing if you have any questions, if you need clarification of the terms and conditions of the contract, or if any disputes occur with the contractor. This delegation of authority is limited to the contract and may not be redelegated by you. You are asked to notify the contracting officer as soon as possible if you cannot continue as the COTR, and this delegation will be terminated in writing immediately.

Receipt acknowledged:

_____ Date_____
COTR's signature

Attachment: Copy of contract number _____

The contractor also must be notified in writing that a COTR has been appointed to serve as a technical expert and as the authorized representative of the contracting officer. The contractor should be sent a copy of the delegation memorandum and must be notified in writing immediately if the COTR appointment is terminated. The notification must specify the effective date of the termination. The written notification may be issued through a modification to the contract, if the contract is still in progress, or as a separate document.

THE COTR'S DUTIES AND RESPONSIBILITIES

A COTR plays a critical role in the outcome of the contract administration process. He or she is appointed to act on behalf of the contracting officer as an authorized representative of the government but does not have the authority to enter into contractual agreements or make changes to contracts. The COTR's authority is limited to performing administrative and technical functions. The COTR's duties and responsibilities may be rather simple for less complex contacts but more involved and time-consuming for large, technically complex contracts.

A COTR must be a federal employee, unless otherwise authorized by agency regulation, because many of the COTR's duties and responsibilities fall in the area of inherently governmental functions (see FAR 7.503(c) for a list of acquisition activities considered to be inherently governmental functions).

Understanding Contract Terms and Conditions

Once a COTR is formally appointed, it is his or her responsibility to read and understand the terms and conditions of the assigned contract. It is extremely important for the COTR to know the scope and limitations of the authority delegated to him or her so that he or she can avoid making unauthorized commitments. To ensure that both the contractor and the COTR understand the requirements and terms and conditions of the contract, contracting officers sometimes hold a postaward conference, sometimes called a *kickoff meeting* or *pre-performance meeting*. For less complex contracts, the necessary information, including any requirements that require the contractor's special attention, may be provided in writing instead of at a formal meeting.

For contracts that require extensive monitoring, the contracting officer may establish necessary administrative procedures for the COTR and contractor to follow. These procedures often apply to the following administrative functions:

- ◆ The invoice payment process

- ◆ Setting the content and frequency of progress reports

- ◆ Determining the types of contract files to be maintained by the COTR and the contractor

- ◆ Establishing communication channels and lines of authority for the government and the contractor

- ◆ Controlling and maintaining government property furnished to the contractor

- ◆ Other administrative issues believed to be in the best interest of the government.

Proprietary Information

The COTR also must review and become familiar with information in the awarded contract considered to be proprietary. Although the COTR is primarily responsible for inspecting or rejecting work under the contract and advising the contactor on technical matters, he or she is also responsible for protecting proprietary information.

Prior to award, information marked as proprietary that is submitted to the government by proposing vendors is subject to protection under the Freedom of Information Act. Once awarded, proprietary information in the contract loses that protection unless it is properly marked as proprietary. Technical data in contracts that are properly marked are protected by the insertion of a clause in FAR 52.227-14, Rights in Data General. If this clause is not included, the data may not be protected.

Monitoring Performance and Handling Problems

The COTR must ensure that the contract requirements are performed as agreed upon by both parties and that the requirements are in compliance with the terms and conditions of the contract. Problems will develop if the contractor does not perform the work in accordance with the contract requirements. The COTR must take immediate action to alert the contracting officer when he or she learns that problems have developed or the contractor is not performing adequately. It is extremely important for the COTR and contracting officer to promptly resolve contract problems because they can lead to costly, time-consuming contract claims against the government.

It is not appropriate for the COTR to advise the contractor on how to correct its performance deficiencies. The contractor has an obligation to communicate at least weekly with the COTR regarding its progress and any problems that develop. Nevertheless, contractors sometimes do not report problems immediately. This often results in additional cost to the government and sometimes extends the period of performance because the government cannot respond to problems promptly if it does not know about them.

Tasks Performed by the COTR

For most agencies, civilian and defense, a COTR's contract administration duties and responsibilities include, at a minimum, the following:

- ◆ Assisting the contracting officer with postaward orientation when asked

- ◆ Recommending to the contracting officer that government-furnished property be provided if needed

- ◆ Monitoring the acquisition, maintenance, and disposition of government-furnished equipment

- ◆ Responding to technical questions or concerns that surface during the period of performance

- Clarifying technical matters for the contractor when asked or as necessary

- Monitoring the contractor's performance and progress to ensure that the terms and conditions of the contract are being fulfilled by the contractor

- Notifying the contracting officer, preferably in writing, when performance, progress, or both are not in compliance with the terms and conditions of the contract

- Receiving, inspecting, and accepting or rejecting all supplies and services received under the contract

- Notifying the contracting officer of any delays in the delivery of supplies or services

- Attending all sessions of equipment testing, whether the equipment is commercial-off-the-shelf or designed and built by the contractor

- Recommending contract modifications based on review of the existing contract

- Recommending the exercise of options (if included in the contract)

- Preparing receiving reports for accepted supplies or services and sending the reports promptly to the designated offices or personnel by the deadline specified in agency rules and regulations.

- Reviewing and approving invoices for payment received from the contractor and submitting them to the contracting officer for processing of payment

- Assisting the contracting officer with any contract claims submitted by the contractor

◆ Preparing all contract completion statements and forms required by the FAR and by agency regulation when the contract is completed.

Recommending Changes

Changes to the scope of work and terms and conditions of contracts are inevitable. When they have to be made, they must be made through contract modifications. A COTR does not have actual authority to bind the government or make changes to the contract, but he or she can *recommend* that modifications be made to the contract when necessary. The COTR is in the best position to make this type of recommendation to the contracting officer because he or she has in-depth knowledge of the contract and the contractor's performance.

The COTR must notify the contracting officer immediately when a contractor makes a request to make changes to the contract. Quite often, these change requests are due to developments unforeseen at the time of contract award. The COTR is responsible for reviewing the contract to ensure that the contractor's request is within the general scope of the contract and for making the appropriate recommendation to the contracting officer. If the requested changes are within the general scope of the contract and are necessary, the contracting officer will proceed with the contract modification process. Changes to a contract must be signed off by the contracting officer or the contracting officer and the contractor before the contractor implements the changes. If the changes materially depart from the scope of the existing contract, the full and open competition requirements must be applied.

Regardless of how diligent the COTR is in monitoring the contractor's performance, changes to the contract might occur before a formal modification to a contract is issued. Work performed beyond a contract's requirements might be the result of an informal government request without a contract modification, or it could be due to the inaction or negative conduct of the COTR. For example, a COTR might request that several testing sessions on hardware be delivered to the government, even though the contract calls for only one test-ing. The COTR's request would cause the contractor to incur extra expenses because it would have to devote more time and possibly additional personnel to perform the testing. In this situation, the con-tractor would probably request monetary compensation through an *equitable adjustment* to the contract, which contractors are entitled to when they are asked to perform work beyond the government's requirements.

Again, the contracting officer is the sole person authorized to enter into contractual agreements and make changes to contracts. The COTR is prohibited from making changes in the following areas of the contract:

♦ Scope of work

♦ Contract price

♦ Supplies or services to be delivered

♦ Quantity of supplies or services

♦ Delivery date for supplies or services

♦ Technical specifications

♦ Contract delivery schedules

♦ Period of performance for the base year and any option years

♦ Administrative provisions.

Unnecessary Interference with Contractor Work

The COTR is obligated not to interfere unnecessarily with the con-tractor's work and not to disrupt or cause delays in the contractor's performance. The COTR must respect the contractor's right to per-form the work without any interference. When this right is violated, a breach of contract occurs. The contractor is legally entitled to the recovery of costs incurred for damages suffered as a result of the breach. A contractor may request an equitable adjustment to its contract if the COTR:

- Interferes with the contractor's performance

- Does not cooperate with the contractor

- Delays the contractor's work performance

- Asks the contractor to accelerate contract performance

- Provides an incorrect interpretation of the contract requirements to the contractor

- Fails to acknowledge defective specifications

- Does not disclose superior knowledge or fails to provide technical information to the contractor

- Uses inspection standards that are higher than those specified in the contract.

Progress Reports

After the contract is awarded, the government will implement the quality assurance plan provided in the contract. This plan, based on the work outlined in the statement of work, should cover the most critical and essential elements of the contract work. The government may use any method of contract monitoring.

COTRs usually develop quarterly or monthly progress reports to keep the contracting officer informed on the progress of the contactor's performance. The complexity and dollar threshold of the contract normally dictate whether a quarterly or a monthly report will be issued. The COTR must relay all information that may affect the contract requirements as quickly as possible to the contracting officer. Contracts usually identify the type and content of the reports the COTR is expected to prepare and submit to the contracting officer.

Monthly Progress Reports

A monthly progress report, rather than a quarterly report, is usually required for complex and high-dollar contracts. A monthly progress report should cover only the most essential elements of contract monitoring. A brief but comprehensive monthly report can be prepared more quickly than a lengthy report, which may ease the contracting officer's and COTR's significant workloads. A monthly report can be read more quickly than a quarterly report covering three months of the contractor's progress and performance.

The monthly progress report should highlight the contractor's technical progress, as well as any potential or actual problems that must be addressed. It should, at a minimum, cover the following:

◆ Observations from visits to the contract site and reasons for the visit (for large, complex contracts; site visits may be made only as necessary for small, simpler contracts)

◆ Technical directions and clarifications given to the contractor

◆ The contractor's progress and performance

◆ Inspection of supplies or services

◆ Results of acceptance testing performed by the contractor, when applicable

◆ Contractor's technical progress reports submitted to the COTR

◆ Contractor's financial status report submitted to the COTR

◆ Deliveries of supplies or services

◆ Invoices reviewed and approved.

Quarterly Progress Reports

For small-dollar and non-complex contracts, a quarterly report works well for reporting contract status because fewer complicated functions are performed during a three-month period for smaller contracts. The quarterly progress report should cover, at a minimum, the following:

- ◆ Progress and performance of the contractor
- ◆ Supplies or services received
- ◆ Invoices reviewed and approved.

A contract administration checklist prepared by the contracting officer and accepted by the COTR will often help in preparing the report.

The COTR should always perform monitoring with care; if not, the contractor could claim that the COTR interfered in its performance of the contract. Unnecessary government interference often leads to disputes and claims by the contractor. Cautious contract monitoring that is properly documented is the key to successful contract completion.

CHAPTER 20

Contract Surveillance

(FAR 16.3, 16.6, 37.6, 42.11, 46.2, 46.4, and 46.601)

Contract surveillance is the monitoring, inspection, and testing of a contractor's work after the contract is awarded and before the government accepts the work. It is done to ensure that quality supplies or services are delivered in a timely manner to the government. Inspection can be carried out by inspecting the actual work performed or by conducting surveillance of the contractor's inspection system. Contract surveillance begins when a contract is awarded, and it does not end until the work under the contract has been completed and accepted or the contract has been terminated.

In March 2005, the Government Accountability Office reviewed 90 contracts for one large agency and found that surveillance was insufficient for 26 of the contracts. Fifteen of the 26 contracts had no surveillance activity, and 11 contracts had no surveillance documentation even though surveillance personnel had been assigned. In January 2007, one agency's inspector general reviewed 24 contracts and found that 23 had inadequate government surveillance. When the government does not have adequate contracting surveillance, it is at risk of being unable to identify and correct poor contractor performance. Assigning properly trained personnel to contracts is one way of mitigating some of the risks.

SURVEILLANCE IS A FUNCTION OF CONTRACT ADMINISTRATION

The terms *contract surveillance* and *contract administration* are sometimes used interchangeably by the federal government, but they have different meanings. Contract administration is far broader, encompassing much more of the acquisition process. Contract surveillance is generally limited to inspection and testing of supplies and services. Contract surveillance, or *production surveillance*, as it is called in the FAR, is a function of contract administration. It involves the government's review and analysis of the contractor's performance. FAR 42.1101 defines production surveillance as follows:

> Production surveillance is a function of contract administration used to determine contractor progress and to identify any factors that may delay performance. Production surveillance involves Government review and analysis of—
> (a) Contractor performance plans, schedules, controls, and industrial processes; and
> (b) The contractor's actual performance under them.

REQUIRED INSPECTION CLAUSES AND QUALITY REQUIREMENTS

The government's goal is for all contracts, whether they are for supplies, services, or construction, to be performed in a timely manner. To encourage progress and efficiency and to protect the government's interest, the FAR requires that inspection requirements and quality assurance requirements be included in all contracts. Per FAR 46.102, agencies must ensure that:

> (a) Contracts include inspection and other quality requirements, including warranty clauses when appropriate, that are determined necessary to protect the Government's interest;
> (b) Supplies or services tendered by contractors meet contract requirements;

(c) Government contract quality assurance is conducted before acceptance (except as otherwise provided in this part), by or under the direction of Government personnel;

(d) No contract precludes the Government from performing inspection;

(e) Nonconforming supplies or services are rejected, except as otherwise provided in 46.407;

(f) Contracts for commercial items shall rely on a contractor's existing quality assurance system as a substitute for compliance with Government inspection and testing before tender for acceptance unless customary market practices for the commercial item being acquired permit in-process inspection (Section 8002 of P.L. 103-355). Any in-process inspection by the Government shall be conducted in a manner consistent with commercial practice; and

(g) The quality assurance and acceptance services of other agencies are used when this will be effective, economical, or otherwise in the Government's interest (see Subpart 42.1).

The mandatory contract quality requirements are contained in the standard inspection clauses in FAR 52.246-1 through 52.246-14. These inspection clauses, except for FAR 52.246-1, must be included in solicitations and contracts for applicable acquisitions in excess of the simplified acquisition threshold of $150,000. The clauses are lengthy, so they should be included only by reference in solicitations and contracts.

These standard inspection clauses give the government the right to make inspections and perform tests while the work of the contractor is in progress. Inspections made while a contractor is performing work must not interfere with the work or cause unnecessary delays.

Agencies most frequently use the two standard inspection clauses for supplies and services under fixed-price contracts. These provide the government broad, comprehensive rights to inspect the work of a contractor. Paragraph (c) of FAR 52.246-2 (Inspection of Supplies—Fixed-Price) states:

> The Government has the right to inspect and test all supplies called for by the contract, to the extent practicable, at all places and times, including the period of manufacture, and in any event before acceptance. The Government shall perform inspections and tests in a manner that will not unduly delay the work. The Government assumes no contractual obligation to perform any inspection and test for the benefit of the Contractor unless specifically set forth elsewhere in this contract.

Paragraph (c) of FAR 52.246-4 (Inspection of Services—Fixed-Price) states:

> The Government has the right to inspect and test all services called for by the contract, to the extent practicable at all times and places during the term of the contract. The Government shall perform inspections and tests in a manner that will not unduly delay the work.

THE COTR'S ROLE IN CONTRACT SURVEILLANCE

The COTR plays a very important role in surveillance. He or she is primarily responsible for inspecting, testing, and approving or rejecting supplies or services provided by the contractor. The contracting officer has a legal responsibility to ensure that the COTR properly performs his or her surveillance duties so that the work is completed on time and meets the quality requirements specified in the contract.

If the government performs proper contract surveillance, it will receive quality supplies or services on time and within budget. If the COTR is not properly trained or his or her surveillance responsibilities are not clearly defined, his or her ability to perform surveillance may be compromised. Poor contract surveillance often leads to poor contractor performance, cost overruns, and delays in receiving the supplies and services.

Several studies and reports have shown that contract surveillance is a weak link in civilian and defense agencies' acquisition processes. The findings indicate that more resources and time are allocated to awarding contracts than to the contract administration phase, especially surveillance. Even if resources are lacking, a properly trained COTR with well-defined responsibilities can perform adequate contract surveillance throughout the duration of the contract.

INSPECTION AND TESTING

When the government acquires commercial supplies or services, it must rely on the contractor's current quality assurance requirements. The contractor is not required to perform inspection and testing of supplies and services for acquisitions at or below the simplified acquisition threshold of $150,000 unless the contracting officer determines that there is a need to do so. When inspection or testing are deemed necessary for an acquisition at or below the threshold of $100,000, the contracting officer must insert FAR 52.246-1 (Contractor Inspection Requirements) in the solicitation and contract.

The government is not required to perform inspection or testing for commercial acquisitions before accepting the supplies or services. Nonetheless, the government has the right to inspect or test any supplies or services that are offered for acceptance.

In addition to the standard inspection and testing clauses required by the FAR, the federal government may develop its own provisions for large and complex contracts or when the contracting officer determines that it is necessary.

See Exhibit 20-1 for a sample agency-developed inspection and testing provision. This sample can be modified to fit any federal government contract. The sample document is requesting the contractor to implement an inspection system and also to perform inspections. It includes a provision that calls for the government to perform inspections during working hours and to notify the contractor 24 hours before arriving on-site. The sample also indicates that the government intends to perform one final inspection upon completion of the work. This inspection must be conducted within a reasonable amount of time after the government has been notified that the work is complete.

EXHIBIT 20-1: Sample Agency-Developed Inspection and Testing Provision

(Sample language that may be included in a contract in addition to one of the standard inspection clauses required by the FAR. Include in section E (Inspection and Acceptance) when using the uniform contract format.)

E-1. Quality assurance: inspection and testing

a. The contractor shall implement an appropriate inspection system to be included in the contractor's quality assurance plan. This plan shall also include a checklist of duties, including inspection and testing, to be performed by the contractor's quality assurance specialist. Inspections shall be performed on a weekly basis (if not weekly, specify other time frames) to determine whether the requirements *(if necessary, specify the work the requirements apply to)* are being performed according to the terms and conditions of the contract. The contractor shall provide an original copy of the weekly inspection report to the government COTR.

b. The contractor shall correct any defects or errors found during the inspection period and before the work is accepted. Any defects or errors for which the contractor is not responsible shall be brought to the attention of the COTR and the contracting officer within 24 hours from the time the defects or errors are found. The contracting officer shall take any necessary action to address defects or errors.

c. In addition to the contractor's inspections, the government will conduct a series of inspections during the performance of the work and one final inspection upon completion of the work. The government shall notify the contractor that an inspection will be performed at least 24 hours before arriving at the contract performance site.

Because the government has broad rights regarding the timing of inspections, it almost never specifies the exact time an inspection will be conducted. Despite its broad rights, the government must take care in performing inspections while the contractor is performing contract work. It is absolutely essential for the government to scrutinize contract work during the performance period so that defects or errors can be discovered early and corrective action can be taken before acceptance. Inspection prior to acceptance is necessary because the government may have limited rights after it accepts the work.

The contractor has the right to submit a claim for an equitable adjustment to the contract if the government conducts an inspection at a time that is unreasonable or causes delays by making an inspection.

The Contractor's Quality Control Measures

Inspection and testing performed by the government is for the benefit of the government. The government is not obligated to perform any inspections or testing for the contractor. The contractor is responsible for establishing its own quality control measures and making sure that the supplies or services it delivers comply with the contract requirements.

The contractor bears responsibility if its work is found to be nonconforming after it is completed because the contractor did not inspect or test it. In cases like this, the government has three options. It can:

♦ Reject the work and ask the contractor to promptly replace the nonconforming supplies or perform the rejected services again.

♦ Reject the work and replace or fix the supplies or perform the services and charge the cost to the contractor.

♦ Initiate default termination proceedings.

The government is not obligated to pay for nonconforming supplies or services if they have been properly rejected, and the contractor is not entitled to be paid the contract price.

Inspection and Receiving Reports

FAR 46.601 requires federal agencies to prescribe procedures and instructions for the use, preparation, and distribution of inspection and receiving reports and commercial shipping documents or packing lists as evidence of inspection.

These inspection and receiving reports are usually summarized, not detailed, in the COTR's progress report, so they are often overlooked by the contracting officer and other acquisition managers who need to know how the contract is progressing. Therefore, it is imperative that COTRs detail the inspection and receiving reports in the body of the progress report or attach them to the progress report. At a minimum, information given on inspection and acceptance in a monthly or quarterly report should include the following:

◆ The date of the inspection

◆ The contractor's company name

◆ A listing of items that were inspected and accepted

◆ A confirmation of inspection by the COTR.

Certificates of Conformance

Under certain circumstances, the government may decide not to inspect supplies or services, instead relying on a *certificate of conformance* provided by the contractor. This certificate may be used only if the contracting officer determines that:

◆ It is in the best interest of the government;

◆ The government would incur minor losses if there were defects;

◆ Based on the contractor's past performance, the supplies or services are likely to be acceptable; and

◆ All defective deliverables would be replaced, corrected, or repaired without any dispute from the contractor.

The contractor must be authorized in writing by the contracting officer to use a certificate of conformance. The contractor then submits the signed certificate with the deliverables. The required text for a certificate of conformance appears in FAR 52.246-15(d):

> I certify that on _____ [*insert date*], the _____ [*insert Contractor's name*] furnished the supplies or services called for by Contract No._____ via _____ [*Carrier*] on _____ [*identify the bill*

of lading or shipping document] in accordance with all applicable requirements. I further certify that the supplies or services are of the quality specified and conform in all respects with the contract requirements, including specifications, drawings, preservation, packaging, packing, marking requirements, and physical item identification (part number), and are in the quantity shown on this or on the attached acceptance document.
Date of Execution:
Signature:
Title:

The government has a right to reject any defective supplies or services within a reasonable period of time after delivery and must notify the contractor in writing of the rejection.

THE CONTRACTOR'S PRODUCTION PROGRESS REPORT

Federal government contracts almost always have provisions that require contractors to submit production progress reports. These reports, commonly called *monthly progress reports*, are not required by regulation but are permitted when the contracting officer determines that they are necessary.

When production progress reporting is required, the contracting officer must insert FAR clause 52.242-2 (Production Progress Reports), shown below, in the contract. This clause is not required for construction or Federal Supply Schedule contracts.

(a) The Contractor shall prepare and submit to the Contracting Officer the production progress reports specified in the contract Schedule.

(b) During any delay in furnishing a production progress report required under this contract, the Contracting Officer may withhold from payment an amount not exceeding $25,000 or 5 percent of the amount of this contract, whichever is less.

If the contract mandates production progress reporting, the contracting officer must also include the appropriate reporting instructions in section E of the uniform contract format. Exhibit 20-2 shows two samples of progress reporting requirements, one detailed and one brief, developed by an agency. These provisions are included in addition to the mandatory FAR clause 52.242-2. The contracting officer may also provide a progress report template to be completed by the contractor.

EXHIBIT 20-2: Sample Contractor's Progress Reporting Requirements

Sample 1
This text should be inserted in section F (Deliveries or Performance) of the uniform contract format.

F-1. Reports

Monthly progress reports
The contractor shall submit performance reports summarizing the progress of the major contract requirements in process. The reports shall specify problems encountered and recommend remedial actions as appropriate.

1. The progress reports shall be submitted on the last working day at the end of each month.

2. The contractor shall submit the reports to the designated COTR identified in section G (Contract Administration Data) of the contract. The COTR is responsible for submitting the reports to the contracting officer responsible for the contract.

3. The contractor shall promptly notify the contracting officer by telephone or email of any problems, delays, or adverse conditions that have prevented the contractor from meeting the requirements of the contract. This communication shall be followed up in writing.

4. The contracting officer shall use the monthly progress reports and input from the COTR to evaluate the contractor's performance on work that has been completed. A copy of the evaluation report shall be submitted to the contactor for review and comments.

5. The contractor will have 30 days from receipt of the evaluation report to comment on the evaluation. If the report is acceptable to the contractor, the contractor shall indicate agreement by signing and returning the evaluation report to the contracting officer.

EXHIBIT 20-2: Sample Contractor's Progress Reporting Requirements (cont.)

Sample 2

This text should be inserted in section E (Inspection and Acceptance) of the uniform contract format.

E-1. Monthly reports

The contractor shall submit a monthly progress report to the COTR along with its monthly invoice. The report shall summarize the contractor's progress, the results of the contractor's inspections, any difficulties or irregularities encountered, corrective actions taken to resolve problems, and any recommendations for improving the conditions of the contract.

Most agencies require contractors to submit progress reports on a monthly basis for high-dollar, highly technical, and complex contracts. Quarterly reports are the norm for simpler or small-dollar contracts.

The COTR is responsible for communicating with the contractor to ensure that the reports are prepared and submitted in accordance with the contract reporting provisions. Monthly progress reports are normally submitted to both the contracting officer and the COTR but may be submitted only to the COTR at the request of the contracting officer. The COTR usually briefs the contracting officer if he or she does not receive a copy of the progress report.

The contractor's progress report should be brief but comprehensive and should summarize the progress made on the contract. It must include only information that is essential to the needs of the government.

To identify any deficiencies or weaknesses in the contractor's progress, the COTR must read the report promptly and closely. Contractors sometimes gloss over problems that can be easily overlooked if the report is not read thoroughly. The COTR must also verify the accuracy of the report, either by thorough review if it or through daily surveillance of the contractor's performance. Any discrepancies found in the report must be brought to the attention of the contracting officer for corrective action.

Sometimes, contractors describe the progress they have made but do not map it to the planned performance schedule outlined in the contract. Progress must always be mapped to the planned performance schedule to ensure that the work is on schedule. When this mapping is omitted, the COTR should ask the contractor to map its progress, or he or she can do the mapping.

When work is not progressing according to the contract schedule, contractors usually identify the parts of the project that are lagging behind and make recommendations for bringing them back on schedule. Sometimes this calls for additional staff and funding, which increases the contract cost. If unforeseen technical difficulties have caused the contractor to fall behind, the government adds the funding needed and extends the period of performance.

CHAPTER 21

Exercising Contract Option Periods

(FAR 16.5 and 6, 17.107, 17.2, 32.703, 42.15, and 52.217-3 through 52.217-9)

Option periods, sometimes called *option years*, give the government a unilateral right to purchase additional supplies or services by extending the period of performance for a contract. The presence of option periods in a contract does not mean that the government is obligated to exercise them. Option periods simply give the government the right to extend the contract period of performance.

When an option period is exercised, it must be in exact compliance with the option provision in the contract. To ensure fair treatment of the contractor, the contractor must be notified within the time period specified in the contract that an option will be exercised. Option periods must also be implemented in a timely manner to prevent any unnecessary delays for the contractor. When an option is exercised, the contractor is responsible for fulfilling the terms and conditions of the contract by delivering the supplies or services to the government, just as it did during the base year.

Bid protest reports have revealed that some federal agencies have exercised out-of-scope option periods. Sometimes, the required option clauses were not included in contracts, and contractors were not notified within the time frame stated in the contract that the government wanted to exercise an option. Acquisition professionals are encouraged to become familiar with the purpose of and procedures for exercising contract option periods.

BENEFITS AND LIMITATIONS OF OPTION PERIODS

The government uses options freely because they are not legally binding. Option clauses do not *require* the government to extend the contract period of performance to purchase additional quantities of supplies or services.

Benefits of Contract Options

The use of contract options gives the federal government some flexibility. Including option clauses in contracts is a way of obtaining firm commitments from vendors to perform additional work and lock in prices before they can escalate in the commercial marketplace. Priced option periods that have been negotiated for the initial contract protect the government from future economic uncertainties in the commercial marketplace. It is more cost-effective to extend the contract period of performance than to go through another costly solicitation and contract award process.

Option periods may be included in solicitation provisions and in contract clauses for both methods of contracting, sealed bidding and contracting by negotiation. Before including an option provision in a solicitation, the contracting officer is required to determine whether it is likely that the option periods will be exercised. Option periods should not be included in a solicitation if there is any question on whether there is a reasonable likelihood that the government will exercise them. When using the sealed bidding method of contracting, the contracting officer must declare in writing that there is a reasonable likelihood that the options will be exercised. A written determination is not required for the negotiated method of contracting.

It makes good business sense to use option periods for large and complex contracts because they do not require the contractor to overcome a new learning curve. What is meant by good business sense? In this case, it means that both the government and the contractor accrue benefits by legally extending a contract to acquire additional supplies or services without incurring additional costs. Option periods also allow the business relationship established between the contractor and the government in the first year of the contract to continue.

It is extremely important for the government to develop a proper working relationship with the contractor in the initial stage of the contract administration phase. If the business relationship between the parties is less than satisfactory, the government could find itself at a disadvantage if it is compelled to exercise an option period to meet critical needs. Weak business relationships often result in production delays, disputes that end up in contract claims, and sometimes poor contractor performance. The business relationship between the government and contractor should always be at arm's length, but it must also be cooperative.

Limitations on the Use of Contract Options

Because there are few limitations on the use of options, they are used widely within the federal acquisition community. However, there are some limitations: Federal agencies do not use options for some contracts, and the FAR does not recommend the use of options when doing so is not in the best interest of the government.

The federal government normally does not include option periods in the following types of contracts, although the FAR does not preclude their use:

- ◆ Construction, alteration, or repair of buildings

- ◆ Architect-engineer

- ◆ Research and development.

Option periods are not necessary for certain requirements. FAR 17.202(b) lists the following circumstances in which the use of options is not in the best interest of the government if the contracting officer determines that:

(1) The foreseeable requirements involve—
(i) Minimum economic quantities (i.e., quantities large enough to permit the recovery of startup costs and the production of the required supplies at a reasonable price); and
(ii) Delivery requirements far enough into the future to permit competitive acquisition, production, and delivery.
(2) An indefinite quantity or requirements contract would be more appropriate than a contract with options. However, this does not preclude the use of an indefinite quantity contract or requirements contract with options.

FAR 17.202(b)(2) states that two types of indefinite-delivery contracts may include option periods: requirements and indefinite-quantity. Large, complex indefinite-quantity contracts with performance periods of three years or less often include option years. But when these two types of contracts are not complex and have small dollar thresholds, option periods are usually not included. This is because the government can issue *task orders* against the contracts to purchase supplies or services as the need arises. Issuing task orders is a much simpler process than exercising option periods. It is advisable to include the agency's ordering procedures in these types of contracts when option periods are used.

The contracting officer may include option periods in solicitations and contracts when doing so is in the best of the government but may not include them under the conditions specified in FAR 17.202(c):

(1) The contractor will incur undue risks; e.g., the price or availability of necessary materials or labor is not reasonably foreseeable;
(2) Market prices for the supplies or services involved are likely to change substantially; or
(3) The option represents known firm requirements for which funds are available unless—
(i) The basic quantity is a learning or testing quantity; and
(ii) Competition for the option is impracticable once the initial contract is awarded.

SOLICITATION PROVISIONS AND CONTRACT CLAUSES

Every solicitation and contract that indicates that the federal government anticipates the contractor to perform additional work must have a provision that provides information on contract option periods. The solicitation and resulting contract must clearly state that the government intends to obtain additional quantities of supplies or extend the period of performance. When option periods are contemplated, the government must include the appropriate option provisions and clauses per FAR 17.208. Sometimes contracting officers include option provisions they have developed in addition to the FAR option provisions and clauses when the government anticipates obtaining additional work by extending the contract period of performance.

When option provisions are included in solicitations, proposing vendors must be told whether the option periods will be evaluated during the initial proposal evaluation period or before exercising each option. The solicitation must also state that the government anticipates exercising the option periods. The option clause in the resulting contract must specify the amount or dollar value of the supplies or services that can be purchased in each option period. The contract clause must also specify the time period during which the option period may be exercised.

Option Provisions for Solicitations

When it is determined that it is appropriate to include option periods in a particular solicitation, the following FAR option provisions must be included:

- ◆ **FAR 52.217-3, Evaluation Exclusive of Options.** Include if options are not to be exercised at time of award, the contract is not firm fixed-price or other type of agency approved contract, and there is a reasonable likelihood that the option will be exercised.

- ◆ **FAR 52.217-4, Evaluation of Options Exercised at Time of Contract Award.** Include if the contracting officer determines it is appropriate to exercise the option at the time of award.

- ◆ **FAR 52.217-5, Evaluation of Options.** Include if the solicitation has an option provision, but the option will *not* be exercised at the time of award, is not a firm-fixed-price contract or other type of agency-approved contract, and there is a reasonable likelihood the option will be exercised.

Option Clauses for Contracts

Option clauses included in contracts must identify the time frame in which the option periods will be exercised. The following FAR option clauses must be included in all solicitations and resulting contracts:

- ◆ **FAR 52.217-6, Option for Increased Quantity.** Include if the government anticipates increasing the quantities of the items at the same price identified in the contract unless agreed differently by the parties. This option is not used for services.

- ◆ **FAR 52.217-7, Option for Increased Quantity—Separately Priced Line Item.** Include if the government anticipates delivery of specific line items at the same price identified in the contract schedule unless agreed differently by the parties. This option is not used for services.

- ◆ **FAR 52.217-8, Option to Extend Services.** Include if the government anticipates continuing any of the services at the same labor (price) rates listed in the schedule. The option period may be exercised more than once, but it may not exceed six months, and the labor rates may be adjusted only if the prevailing rates are adjusted by the secretary of Labor.

- ◆ **FAR 52.217-9, Option to Extend the Term of the Contract.** Include if the government anticipates extending the contract period of performance by exercising the option. The contractor must be given a preliminary notice at least 60 days, maybe less, from expiration of the contract.

Sample Option Provisions and Clauses

The solicitation provisions and contract clauses for option periods provided in FAR 17.208 may be used when using the uniform contract format (UCF) or the commercial contract format. The FAR option provisions and clauses must be included in part II, section I (Contract Clauses) when using the UCF. Option provisions developed by the government usually supplement the information in the FAR provisions and clauses. Unless agency regulation dictates otherwise, agency-developed provisions should be included in part I, section F (Deliveries or Performance), when using the UCF. Exhibit 21-1 shows a sample agency-developed option provision. FAR clauses 52.217-8 and 52.217-9, which are identified in the agency-developed provision in Exhibit 21-1, appear in full text in Exhibits 21-2 and 21-3.

EXHIBIT 21-1: Sample Agency-Developed Option Provision

Insert in part I, section F (Deliveries or Performance) of the uniform contract format.

1. Option Periods

F.2.0. Period of Performance

F.2.1. The performance period for this contract is one base year, with four one-year option periods. The period of performance in the base year includes any transition periods authorized under this contract.

F.2.2. The government may exercise the option periods within the period of performance for this contract as authorized by FAR 52.217-8 (Option to Extend Services). The FAR option clause is provided in full text in section I of this contract.

F.2.3. The government may also extend the term of this contract as authorized by FAR 52.217-9 (Option to Extend the Term of the Contract). The total period of performance for this contract shall not exceed the time period identified in FAR 52.217-9, which is provided in full text in section I of this contract.

EXHIBIT 21-2: FAR Option Clauses for Commercial Contracts

Insert in part (c), section (2) of a commercial contract as an addendum to FAR 52.212-4 (Contract Terms and Conditions—Commercial Items).

52.217-8. Option to Extend Services

The Government may require continued performance of any services within the limits and at the rates specified in the contract. These rates may be adjusted only as a result of revisions to prevailing labor rates provided by the Secretary of Labor. The option provision may be exercised more than once, but the total extension of performance hereunder shall not exceed 6 months. The Contracting Officer may exercise the option by written notice to the Contractor within *(insert the period of time within which the contracting officer may exercise the option).*

(End of clause)

52.217-9. Option to Extend the Term of the Contract

(a) The Government may extend the term of this contract by written notice to the Contractor within *(insert the period of time within which the contracting officer may exercise the option)*, provided that the Government gives the Contractor a preliminary written notice of its intent to extend at least _____ *(insert 60 days, unless a different number of days is required by the agency)* before the contract expires. The preliminary notice does not commit the Government to an extension.

(b) If the Government exercises this option, the extended contract shall be considered to include this option clause.

(c) The total duration of this contract, including the exercise of any options under this clause, shall not exceed *(insert number of months or years).*

(End of clause)

52.212-2. Evaluation—Commercial Items

When option periods are to be evaluated, include this provision in full text in part (e), section (3), of the solicitation when using the format for acquiring commercial items.

EXHIBIT 21-3: FAR Option Clauses for the Uniform Contract Format

Insert in part II, section I (Contract Clauses) when using the uniform contract format.

I.1. 52.217-8—Option to Extend Services

The Government may require continued performance of any services within the limits and at the rates specified in the contract. These rates may be adjusted only as a result of revisions to prevailing labor rates provided by the Secretary of Labor. The option provision may be exercised more than once, but the total extension of performance hereunder shall not exceed 6 months. The Contracting Officer may exercise the option by written notice to the Contractor within *(insert the period of time within which the contracting officer may exercise the option)*.

(End of clause)

I.2. 52.217-9—Option to Extend the Term of the Contract

(a) The Government may extend the term of this contract by written notice to the Contractor within *(insert the period of time within which the contracting officer may exercise the option)*, provided that the Government gives the Contractor a preliminary written notice of its intent to extend at least _____ *(insert 60 days, unless a different number of days is required by the agency)* before the contract expires. The preliminary notice does not commit the Government to an extension.

(b) If the Government exercises this option, the extended contract shall be considered to include this option clause.

(c) The total duration of this contract, including the exercise of any options under this clause, shall not exceed *(insert number of months or years)*.

(End of clause)

When acquiring commercial items, any of the solicitation provisions and contract clauses provided in FAR 17.208 may be used if the contracting officer determines that doing so is in the best interest of the government. If the options are to be evaluated by the procuring agency, FAR 52.212-2 (Evaluation—Commercial Items) must be included, preferably in full text because the provision must be completed by the proposing vendor. According to FAR 12.303(e), FAR 52.212-2 should be included in part (e), section 3, as an addendum when using the contract format for the acquisition of commercial items.

See Exhibit 21-2 for examples of two FAR option clauses that may be included in solicitations and contracts when purchasing commercial items. The two clauses pertain to obtaining additional commercial supplies and extending the term of the contract. The same clauses may be used for acquisitions using the UCF. When using the UCF, the clauses must be included in section I of the contract in full text because the contracting officer is required to include the time periods during which the option may be exercised and the contractor notified about the government's intent to exercise the option.

Because commercial items can be purchased off the shelf, it is not necessary for the contracting officer to develop additional option provisions when acquiring them. The FAR, however, does not prohibit the government from developing additional option provisions for commercial items, so it can be done when doing so would benefit the government and the contractor.

DETERMINING WHETHER TO EXERCISE AN OPTION PERIOD

A contract option period must be exercised before the contract expires. Both the contracting officer and the COTR or the designated official from the program office must determine whether it is necessary and appropriate to exercise an option period before preparing the required documentation. The contracting officer, with some assistance from the COTR, is responsible for performing a preliminary assessment of the contractor's performance and all tasks completed under the contract.

Factors to Consider

When making the required determination of whether to exercise an option period, the two most important factors to take into consideration are:

- ◆ The government's continuing need for the services to be performed

◆ The contractor's past performance record under the existing contract or a previous contract under which similar supplies or services were provided.

The contracting officer may exercise an option period only after determining that:

◆ Government funds are available.

◆ The option period covers the existing needs of the government.

◆ Exercising the option period is the most advantageous way to fulfill the needs of the government.

◆ The option price is equal to or better than prices in the commercial marketplace.

◆ The commercial market is economically stable.

◆ Disrupting contract operations would be costly.

◆ The option was publicized on the governmentwide point of entry (FedBizOpps) and was competed or not competed in accordance with FAR 5.202 exemptions.

◆ The time period between award of the initial contract and exercise of an option is so short that it is evident the option price is the lowest available.

Reviewing the Contractor's Past Performance

The contractor's past performance on the current or a previous contract is among the most important information used by the contracting officer to determine whether it is feasible to exercise an option period. The contracting officer considers the contractor's technical and administrative performance and ability to control costs.

When reviewing the contractor's performance history, the following questions can help the contracting officer determine whether it is beneficial for the government to exercise an option.

- ◆ Did the contract require the contractor to provide a quality assurance plan?

- ◆ Did the contractor submit an acceptable quality assurance plan that was used during contract performance?

- ◆ Did the contractor submit acceptable monthly progress and financial status reports as required by the contract?

- ◆ Did the contractor perform the work in accordance with the contract SOW?

- ◆ Did the contractor try to control contract costs?

- ◆ Did the contractor adhere to the milestone schedule in the contract or as provided by the COTR or contracting officer?

- ◆ Did the contractor deliver the supplies or services in accordance with the schedule in the contract?

- ◆ Did the contractor ever deliver supplies or services late?

- ◆ If equipment testing was required, did the contractor perform acceptable testing within the required time frame?

- ◆ Were there delays in contract performance that were not due to the government's interference?

- ◆ Was the contractor responsible, with quality workmanship and high ethical standards?

- ◆ Was there evidence that the contractor was interested in satisfying the government through good performance?

Taking a positive past performance rating into consideration when making a determination to exercise an option period gives the contractor significant incentive to continue providing high-quality work. The business relationship established during the initial contract period will also continue to benefit the government.

DOCUMENTING THE DETERMINATION

After the contracting officer has reviewed the contract terms, the government's needs, economic factors, and the contractor's past performance, and has determined that is in the best interest of the government to exercise an option period, the following documents must be prepared:

- ◆ A determination and findings

- ◆ A preliminary notice to the contractor of the government's intent to exercise an option

- ◆ A modification to the contract or other written document that notifies the contractor that the option is being exercised.

FAR 17.207(a) and (g) do not require agencies to modify the contract when exercising options. However, it is strongly recommended that the contract be modified when exercising an option period. A unilateral modification signed only by the contracting officer is usually issued for exercising options, but a bilateral modification signed by the contractor and contracting officer may also be issued. Whether it is a modification or a written document, the option clause cited in the contract must be used as the authority for exercising an option period.

Preparing the Determination and Findings

The determination and findings (D&F) must provide facts that will support the determination to exercise an option and must include, at a minimum, the following information:

- ◆ The number of option periods in the contract

- ◆ The duration of the contract period, including all option periods (not to exceed five contract years)

- ◆ The quantity of items to be acquired during the option period, or the amount of time by which performance will be extended

♦ The time frame given for notifying the contractor about exercising the option period

♦ The value of the option to be exercised

♦ Any limitations identified in the contract.

See Exhibit 21-4 for a sample determination and findings for exercising an option period.

EXHIBIT 21-4: Sample Determination and Findings to Exercise an Option Period

(Insert name of agency)
Determination and Findings
Authority to Exercise Option to Extend the Period of Performance

In accordance with FAR 17.207 and the following findings, it has been determined to be in the best interest of the federal government to exercise option period *(insert option number)* to extend the period of performance of the contract.

FINDINGS

1. Background
Contract number _____ was awarded with one base year and *(insert number)* option periods to provide *(type of supplies or services).* The solicitation for the requirements was synopsized in the governmentwide point of entry and was competed under the full and open competition method of contracting. *(If other than full and open competition, state method used to award contract.)* The option periods were evaluated and negotiated in the initial competition.

2. Contractor performance
The contractor's performance on the current contract was evaluated and determined to be satisfactory *(insert other rating if appropriate).* The evaluation indicates that the contractor is meeting the required performance levels and delivery schedule. *(Provide results of evaluation of work on previous contract(s) when appropriate.)*

3. Notice to contractor
Based on the contractor's performance of the contract, a preliminary written notice of the government's intent to exercise option period *(insert option number)* was sent to the contractor on *(date)* as required by the option clause in the contract.

EXHIBIT 21-4: Sample Determination and Findings to Exercise an Option Period (cont.)

4. Price reasonableness

A review of prices in the marketplace for the needed *(insert supplies or services)* indicates that the price for this option period is lower. Based on this review, the option price has been determined to be fair and reasonable. There are no limitations in the contract on the option price that was negotiated in the initial award. *(Other information that may be included: (1) If a new solicitation was issued, indicate whether it produced or failed to produce a better price. (2) Note whether the time period between contract award and exercise of the option is so short that it indicates the option price is the lowest.)*

5. Government's need

The government has a continuing need for the *(identify the supplies or services)* that would be provided during the option period. It is essential that the contractor continue to perform the work and deliver the needed *(insert supplies or services)* in a timely manner. Disruption to operations will be inefficient and costly. Exercising the option is the most advantageous method of meeting the needs of the government at a fair and reasonable price.

6. Funding for the option

The total value of the option period to be exercised is *(dollar amount),* and funds are available, as certified by the financial officer in the *(name of office).*

DETERMINATION

In accordance with FAR 17.207 and *(insert reference to agency regulation on options),* and based upon the findings above, I hereby determine that exercising the option is the most advantageous method of fulfilling the government's needs, price and other factors considered.

_____

Contracting officer *(insert name)*

_____   _____

(Signature)   Date

A D&F for exercising an option period must be approved in accordance with agency regulation or policy. If agency regulation or policy do not specify who should act as the approving official for option periods, the determination and findings should be approved by an individual who is one level above the contracting officer. Obtaining approval from an employee above the contracting officer is one way to keep senior management informed of actions taken to exercise an option period, especially if the contract is complex and high-dollar.

Per FAR 4.803(b)(1), the D&F should be made a part of the contract files. Though paragraph (b)(1) does not specifically identify the D&F as a record that should be made a part of the contract file, it does state that all modifications and supporting documents are normally contained in contract files.

Notifying the Contractor of the Intent to Exercise an Option Period

Per FAR 17.207, the contracting officer must notify the contractor of the government's intent to exercise an option within the time period specified in the contract. The notification to the contractor must be made in writing, either by email or regular mail. (An emailed notification should be followed up with a hard copy sent by regular mail.)

Sometimes agencies notify the contractor more quickly than the contract requires. Every once in a while, contractors are not notified within the specified time period because problems developed at the last minute or the government inadvertently neglected to issue the notification. Reasons the notification might be delayed include:

- The contracting officer forgot to notify the contractor.
- Approval of funding for the option period was delayed by the office that requested the supplies or services.
- The contractor's past performance was still under consideration, even though its performance was satisfactory, because the contractor required constant government supervision when performing contract work.
- The employee administering the contract is new to federal acquisitions and is not aware of the notification requirement.

Contractors should be notified no less than 30 days from expiration of the contract that the government intends to exercise an option period. They must be given reasonable notice so they can assess their resources, both financial and staffing, and can be ready to continue providing the needed supplies or services. When the government intends to extend the term of the contract, the FAR recommends that the contractor be notified at least 60 days before the contract expires, but it allows for a different notification deadline. If notification is made less than 60 days before the contract expires, it is imperative that the contracting officer take into consideration the dollar value and technical complexity of the contract. The 60-day period recommended by the FAR is intended to give the contractor sufficient lead time to continue producing the needed supplies or providing the services. Small-dollar contracts that are not technically complex may require only 30 to 45 days lead time to continue performance.

When an agency is ready to exercise an option, it is very important that it meet all the requirements mandated by the FAR. It may be helpful to have a checklist, such as the sample shown in Exhibit 21-5, that identifies the essential elements that must be addressed prior to exercising an option.

EXHIBIT 21-5: Checklist for Exercising an Option Period			
Contract number _____			
	Actions for exercising option	**Yes/no/NA**	**Date of action**
1.	**Written request from program office before expiration of contract**		
a.	Contract expires in 60 days_____; 90 days _____		
b.	Request to exercise option period _____ for period of performance from _____ to _____ received from program office		
c.	Adequate funds are available		
d.	Contractor performance has been determined to be satisfactory		
e.	SOW requires modification		

	EXHIBIT 21-5: Checklist for Exercising an Option Period (cont.)		
2.	**Determination and findings**		
a.	Prepared in accordance with FAR 17.207		
b.	Prepared in accordance with FAR 6.001(c)		
c.	Prepared in accordance with agency policy		
3.	**Notification to contractor**		
a.	Time frame is specified in the contract for notifying the contractor. Number of days before expiration of contract: _____		
b.	Written notification of intent to exercise option signed by the contracting officer and sent to the contractor by email and regular mail		
4.	**Contract modification or other written document**		
a.	Required modification(s) made to the SOW		
b.	Amount of funds obligated is included		
c.	Accounting and appropriations data are included		
d.	Type of modification (unilateral or bilateral) is specified		
e	The contract option clause is specified as the authority in the modification or written document		
f.	If modification issued, the contractor is required to sign the modification		

RESTRICTIONS ON EXERCISING OPTION PERIODS

Option periods may not be exercised when any of the following conditions exist:

- ◆ The option period has expired.

- ◆ Adequate funds are not available.

- ◆ The government intends to purchase supplies or services that exceed the number of items allowable during the option period to be exercised.

Option periods should not be used to purchase large quantities of items. They are to be used primarily for purchasing additional quantities of supplies or services and to extend the contract period of performance. Purchasing quantities beyond the quantities identified in an option period clearly constitutes a new acquisition. Exercising option periods when funds are not available or when the option periods have expired are invalid exercises. Option periods must be exercised in accordance with the contract option provisions, FAR 17.207 (Exercise of Options) and FAR part 6 (Competition Requirements). To meet the competition requirements, the option exercised must have been evaluated as part of the initial contract competition.

When an option is properly exercised, it turns into an *obligation*, at which time the government must obligate funds for the option period. Funding for option periods must comply with the bona fide needs rule, which requires that a fiscal year appropriation be obligated only to meet a legitimate need that exists or continues to exist in the fiscal year for which the appropriation was made. Therefore, the contracting officer must ensure that funds to be obligated meet a bona fide need of the current fiscal year, not the subsequent fiscal year, before funding an option period.

When exercising an option period, federal agencies must comply with congressional limitations on the use of appropriated funds by ensuring that:

- ◆ The funds are obligated for a proper purpose;
- ◆ The funds are obligated within the time limits applicable to the agency's appropriation; and
- ◆ The obligation is not in excess of the agency's appropriation amount.

A 2006 decision by the Government Accountability Office (GAO) demonstrates what can happen if funds are improperly obligated. Electronic Data Systems was providing services to the National Labor Relations Board (NLRB) under an ongoing operational and technical support contract that was considered to be a severable services contract. (Severable services fulfill the bona fide needs of the fiscal year in which they are performed and cannot cross fiscal years.) GAO found that NLRB violated the bona fide needs rule by funding an option period that began in fiscal year 2006 with expired funds from fiscal year 2005 (B-308026, September 14, 2006). The comptroller general determined that NLRB had improperly obligated its fiscal year 2005 appropriation by using it to fund services that occurred entirely in fiscal year 2006.

Agencies must obligate funds for each option period, but only when the funds are available. The authority to obligate funds expires if an appropriation is not obligated during the period of availability. Because the government may incur new funding obligations only within the period of availability, it is important for the contracting officer to ascertain the duration of the availability period before obligating funds to exercise option periods.

Glossary

Acquisition Career Management Information System: A database managed by the Federal Acquisition Institute that compiles educational and training information on the federal acquisition workforce.

Antideficiency violation: Occurs when a federal agency obligates or expends funds in excess of the amount available in its appropriation or fund if not authorized by law.

Appropriation: Authorization by the U.S. Congress for the federal government to incur obligations and pay for them from the U.S. Treasury.

Appropriations bill: Proposed law also referred to as appropriations legislation to authorize the expenditure of public funds for specific purposes by the federal government.

Best value: The expected outcome of an acquisition that, in the government's estimation, provides the greatest overall benefit in response to the requirements (FAR 2.101).

Bona fide needs rule: Rule allowing an appropriation to be obligated only to meet a legitimate need existing during the appropriation's period of availability.

Buy-in: A proposing vendor's submission of an offer below the government's anticipated cost.

Certificate of competency: A certificate issued by the Small Business Administration that confirms that a small business is a responsible vendor capable of receiving and performing a specific government contract.

Certificate of current cost or pricing data: A specially formatted certificate that a proposing vendor must complete to certify that the cost or pricing data it is submitting to the government is accurate, complete, and current.

Competitive range: A highly ranked group of proposals that have been selected to continue in an acquisition competition based on the rating of all submitted proposals against all evaluation criteria.

Comptroller general: The person appointed to a 15-year term by the president of the United States to manage and direct the Government Accountability Office.

Constructive change: A change, which may be authorized or unauthorized by the government, that occurs when the contract work is changed and the procedures of the changes clause in the contract have not been followed.

Contingency contracting: Emergency contracting to support a military operation. The supplies or services acquired are to be used to facilitate defense against, or recovery from, nuclear, biological, chemical, or radiological attack.

Continuing resolution: A piece of legislation, sometimes called a *spending bill*, that is passed by Congress to allow the federal government to continue operations for a short period of time in the absence of an approved budget.

Contract: A binding legal agreement between a seller, who will furnish supplies or services, and a buyer, who will pay for them. Contracts include awards, task orders under basic ordering agreements, letter contracts, purchase orders, and bilateral contract modifications.

Contractor: A person or other legal entity that is a party to a federal government contract.

Contract award amount: The full potential value of an awarded contract, including the value of the base year plus any option periods.

Contract claim: A written demand made by a contractor seeking monetary relief, the adjustment or interpretation of contract terms, or other kinds of relief arising under or related to a contract. Per the Contract Disputes Act of 1978, a demand for relief exceeding $100,000 must be certified in order for it to be considered a claim.

Contract terms and conditions: Provisions that define how a contract is to be implemented and administered.

Contracting officer: The person delegated the authority to enter into, administer, and terminate federal government contracts.

Contracting officer's representative: A contracting officer's technical representative.

Contracting officer's technical representative: A person designated by a contracting officer to perform contract administration activities that are technical in nature.

Cost analysis: The review and evaluation of each separate cost element in a vendor's proposal, including profit, which is used to determine whether the proposed costs are fair and reasonable, taking into consideration the state of the country's economy.

Cost-plus-a-percentage-of-cost contract: A form of contract in which the amount of fee or profit paid is calculated as a percentage of the actual cost to the vendor of performing the work so that fee or profit increases commensurate with the increases in cost. The federal government is prohibited from using this type of contract by two statutes: 41 USC 254(b) and 10 USC 2306(a).

Cost realism: Situation in which the costs in a proposing vendor's proposal are realistic, indicating that the vendor understands the requirements and that the costs are appropriate for the associated technical proposal.

Cost reasonableness: Situation in which the cost of a contract does not exceed what a prudent person would incur in the competitive marketplace.

Defense Contract Audit Agency (DCAA): A government audit agency that is responsible for performing financial audits on contractors for all federal agencies, except educational institutions and nonprofit organizations.

Determination and findings (D&F): A special form of written approval by an authorized official that is required by statute or regulation before certain contracting actions may be taken. The findings within a D&F support a determination or decision.

Direct costs: Costs, such as direct material and direct labor, that can be traced or charged to a specific job.

Equitable adjustment: An adjustment to a contract price, including profit, under the contract changes clause to recover additional costs incurred when work is changed.

Evaluated option: A contract option that is evaluated for award purposes by adding the total price for the option periods to the total price for the basic year.

Evaluation criteria: Factors and significant sub-factors provided in the solicitaiton for use by the government to evaluate vendor proposals and to select the winning contractor.

FedBizOpps: A website (www. *fbo.gov*) through which the public can electronically access federal government business opportunities greater than $25,000. Often called a *governmentwide point of entry*.

Federal agency: Any executive agency or independent establishment in the legislative or judicial branch of the federal government. The Senate, the House of Representatives, and the Architect of the Capitol are not federal agencies.

Fee: A flat charge paid as compensation for supplies or services provided by a vendor. Fees are associated with cost-reimbursement contracts.

Fiscal year: The federal government's accounting period, which begins October 1 and ends September 30.

Freedom of Information Act: A statute that specifies, among other things, how agencies must provide their records to the public when requested. It imposes strict limits on the amount of time allowed for agency responses and exempts various types of information from public disclosure.

Government Accountability Office (GAO): A federal agency headed by the comptroller general of the United States. Part of the legislative branch, it is charged with investigating all matters that relate to the receipt, disbursement, and use of public funds. GAO is responsible for issuing legal decisions and opinions on appropriations law, bid protests, and other matters that relate to public funds. Its main mission is to improve the performance of the federal government and hold it accountable to Congress and the American public.

Governmentwide point of entry (GPE): An electronic portal, such as FedBizOpps (www. *fbo.gov),* where solicitations, proposed contracts, and other federal government acquisition opportunities over $25,000 are advertised and can be accessed by the public.

Head of the contracting activity: A federal government official who is responsible for the overall management of an agency's contracting activity.

HUBZone small business: A small business that is located in a historically underutilized business zone in an urban or rural area.

Inherently governmental function: A function that is so closely related to the public interest that only federal employees can perform it. These functions fall into two categories: (1) acts of governing and (2) monetary transactions and entitlements.

Inspector general: An officer within each executive department of the federal government who is appointed by the president and charged with performing independent audits and investigating the activities of the department.

Interested party: A vendor that made an offer on a government contract and whose direct economic interest would be affected by the award of the contract.

Liquidated damages: A monetary amount agreed upon by a contractor and the government that must be paid by the contractor if the contractor fails to deliver the supplies or perform the services specified in the contract.

Lump sum estimate: An estimate that does not provide a cost breakdown; rather, it states a single price that includes all cost elements needed to complete the work.

Market research: The collection and analysis of information on vendors, supplies, and services available in the commercial marketplace to determine whether they meet the government's needs.

Members of Congress: Members of the U.S. House of Representatives and U.S. Senate.

Micropurchase: An acquisition of supplies or services, using simplified acquisition procedures, that do not cost more than $3,000.

Nonseverable service: A service that produces a single or a unified outcome that cannot be divided into separate components or performance periods in different fiscal years.

Office of Federal Procurement Policy (OFPP): An office within the Office of Management and Budget that is responsible for establishing the overall direction of federal acquisition policies, procedures, and regulations; providing forms to all federal agencies; and promoting economy, efficiency, and effectiveness in the purchase of supplies and services.

Option period: A specific time period during which the government has a unilateral right to extend the period of performance of a contract to purchase additional supplies or services specified in the contract.

Overhead costs: A company's general operating expenses that may be associated with multiple cost objectives, not traced to one cost objective. Also called *indirect costs.*

Performance work statement (PWS): A statement of work for performance-based acquisitions that describes the required deliverables in definitive and objective terms with measurable outcomes.

Period of availability: The period of time during which an agency appropriation is available for obligation.

Priced option: An option for which the price is specified in the contract or can reasonably be determined from the contract terms of the basic contract, as described in FAR 17.207(f)(1) through (5).

Procurement executive: A federal employee who is responsible for managing an agency acquisition system and implementing acquisition policies, regulations, and standards.

Profit: Within the federal acquisition arena, the additional money a contractor receives above its operating costs.

Protest: A written objection by a vendor objecting to the federal government's solicitation of proposals, cancellation of a solicitation, or award or proposed award of a contract.

Quality assurance plan: A plan that describes how the government will assess the contractor's performance in meeting the performance standards provided in the contract.

Ratification: A process used by an authorized government official to approve an unauthorized commitment made by a government employee who did not have the authority to bind the government.

Request for invitations (RFI): A notice issued to the public by the government to obtain price, delivery, and other market information including vendor capabilities to be used for acquisition planning purposes.

Request for proposals (RFP): An invitation to vendors in the commercial market to submit a proposal for specific supplies or services.

Request for quotations (RFQ): An invitation to vendors in the commercial market to submit price quotes for specific supplies or services.

Requirement: A documented need for supplies or services that identifies the attributes, capabilities, characteristics, or quality of the supplies or services.

Scope of work: The detailed description within a statement of work of the specific services or tasks that a contractor must produce or provide under a contract.

Service-disabled veteran-owned small business: A small company owned by a veteran with a service-related disability.

Severable service: A service that can be separated into components; each component can meet the needs of the government independently.

Simplified acquisition: An acquisition method used by the federal government to purchase supplies or services not exceeding a threshold of $150,000 (commonly called the *simplified acquisition threshold*).

Small Business Administration (SBA): The Small Business Act of 1953 created SBA, an independent agency to aid, counsel, assist, and protect the interests of small business concerns. SBA is also reponsible for ensuring that small business concerns receive a fair share of government contracts and sales of surplus property.

Small business concern: A business entity, including its affiliates, that is independently owned and operated, is certified as a small business, and is not dominant in its field of operation.

Small disadvantaged business: A small company owned and controlled by socially and economically disadvantaged individuals.

Sole source acquisition: A contract for supplies or services that was awarded by an agency after soliciting a proposal from and negotiating with only one vendor.

Source selection: The process used by the government's proposal evaluation team to identify the proposing vendor that will receive a contract in a competitive negotiated acquisition.

Source selection authority: A government employee who is responsible for making the source selection decision, based on his or her independent judgment and the government's proposal evaluation reports.

Special item number (SIN): A numerical designation specified in the Federal Supply Schedule for a group of similar supplies or services that are intended to be used for the same general purpose or function.

Specification: A detailed and precise description of materials, equipment, construction systems, standards, and quality of work that is attached to a contract or solicitation document.

Statement of objectives (SOO): A document prepared by the government that is incorporated into a solicitation and identifies overall performance objectives. A SOO provides vendors the maximum flexibility to propose innovative approaches for the government's requirement.

Statement of work (SOW): The structural framework that defines the contract work to be performed by the contractor and usually includes the contactor's performance standards.

Sustain: As used by the Government Accountability Office, to affirm or approve a protest filed by a disgruntled vendor on the issuance or cancellation of a solicitation or the award or proposed award of a contract.

Technical evaluation panel: A panel of employees who evaluate proposals submitted by vendors for competitive negotiated acquisitions or two-step sealed bidding acquisitions.

Testing: The inspection of an item, including its components, using established scientific principles and procedures to determine whether it works and whether it has defects.

Unbalanced pricing: The understatement or overstatement of individual line item prices in a price proposal.

Unauthorized commitment: An agreement that is not binding because it was made by a government employee who did not have the authority to enter into the agreement on behalf of the government.

Veteran-owned small business: A small company that is at least 51 percent owned and controlled by one or more veterans.

Woman-owned small business: A small company that is at least 51 percent owned and controlled by a woman or women.

Index

R

ranking criteria, 126–127
reductions below maximum threshold, 224
representations and instructions, 111–113
request for information (RFI), 41–42
request for proposal (RFP), 122
requesting office, 21
research and development advance notices, 41
responsibility, determining, 182–185
responsibility requirements, 88
RFI. *See* request for information
RFP. *See* request for proposal

S

SAP. *See* simplified acquisition procedures
SARA. *See* Services Acquisition Reform Act
SBA. *See* Small Business Administration
SBSA. *See* Small Business Set-Aside Program
schedule, 105–108
scope of work, 46
SDVOB. *See* Service-Disabled Veteran-Owned Business
sealed bidding
    awarding contracts, 58
    conditions for, 55–56
    forms used for, 56
    opening, 56–58
    overview, 54–55
    Standard Form 33, 57
    two-step sealed bids, 58–59
Service Contact Act, 48
service contracts, 16
Service-Disabled Veteran-Owned Business (SDVOB), 91
Services Acquisition Reform Act (SARA), 43
set-asides, 88
severable service contracts, 16–17

SF-33. *See* Standard Form 33
significant weakness, 147
simplified acquisition procedures (SAP), 94, 109
simplified acquisition threshold, 163–164
SIN. *See* special item number
size standards, small business program, 85–87
small business, 91
Small Business Act, 84–85, 92, 95–96
Small Business Administration (SBA), 84
small business concern, 84
small business program
    agency small business office responsibilities, 96–99
    certificate of competency, 88
    dollar threshold requirements, 93
    eligibility, 90–91
    exempt acquisitions, 89–90
    HUBZone business, 92
    micropurchases, 93–94
    overview, 83
    partial set-asides, 89
    purpose, 84
    responsibility requirements, 88
    service-disabled veteran-owned small business, 91
    set-asides, 88
    simplified acquisition procedures, 94
    size standards, 85–87
    small business concerns, 84–85
    small disadvantaged business, 92–93
    subcontracting plan requirements, 94–96
    total set-asides, 89
    veteran-owned small business, 91
    woman-owned small business, 93
Small Business Set-Aside Program (SBSA), 88
small disadvantaged business, 92–93
solicitation formats
    commercial items, 113–116
    contract clauses, 108–111

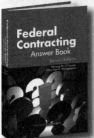

Federal Acquisition ActionPacks

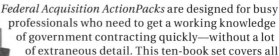

Federal Acquisition ActionPacks are designed for busy professionals who need to get a working knowledge of government contracting quickly—without a lot of extraneous detail. This ten-book set covers all phases of the acquisition process, grounds you firmly in each topic area, and outlines practical methods for success, from contracting basics to the latest techniques for improving performance.

Each spiral-bound book contains approximately 160 pages of quick-reading information—simple statements, bulleted lists, questions and answers, charts and graphs, and more. Each topic's most important information is distilled to its essence, arranged graphically for easy comprehension and retention, and presented in a user-friendly format designed for quick look-up.

> ## Order the full set of Federal Acquisition ActionPacks *to get a comprehensive knowledge of government contracting today.*
> Full set: ISBN 978-1-56726-198-1 ■ Product Code B981

Order the full set or order the single titles that are most important to your role in the contracting process. Either way, this is the most effective, affordable way for both buyers and sellers to get a broad-based understanding of government contracting—and proven tools for success.

Earned Value Management *Gregory A. Garrett* ISBN 978-1-56726-188-2 ■ Product Code B882 173 Pages	**Best-Value Source Selection** *Philip E. Salmeri* ISBN 978-1-56726-193-6 ■ Product Code B936 178 Pages
Performance-Based Contracting *Gregory A. Garrett* ISBN 978-1-56726-189-9 ■ Product Code B899 153 Pages	**Government Contract Law Basics** *Thomas G. Reid* ISBN 978-1-56726-194-3 ■ Product Code B943 175 Pages
Cost Estimating and Pricing *Gregory A. Garrett* ISBN 978-1-56726-190-5 ■ Product Code B905 161 Pages	**Government Contracting Basics** *Rene G. Rendon* ISBN 978-1-56726-195-0 ■ Product Code B950 176 Pages
Contract Administration and Closeout *Gregory A. Garrett* ISBN 978-1-56726-191-2 ■ Product Code B912 153 Pages	**Performance Work Statements** *Philip E. Salmeri* ISBN 978-1-56726-196-7 ■ Product Code B967 151 Pages
Contract Formation *Gregory A. Garrett and William C. Pursch* ISBN 978-1-56726-192-9 ■ Product Code B929 163 Pages	**Contract Terminations** *Thomas G. Reid* ISBN 978-1-56726-197-4 ■ Product Code B974 166 Pages